SAMURAI

The Story of a Warrior Tradition

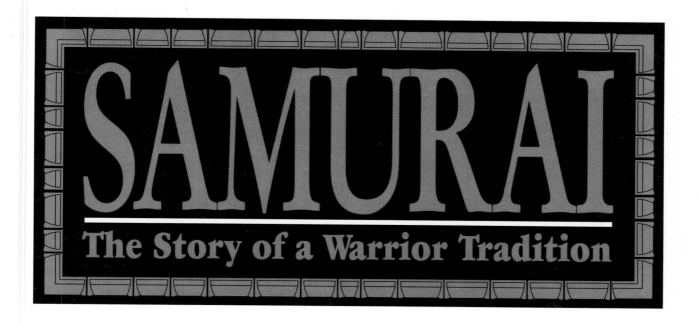

SAMURAI

The Story of a Warrior Tradition

by
Harry Cook

Sterling Publishing Co., Inc.
New York

Library of Congress Cataloging-in-Publication Data Available

This book was edited, designed and produced by Morgan Samuel Editions

First paperback edition published in 1998 by Sterling Publishing Company, Inc
387 Park Avenue South, New York, N.Y. 10016

©1993 by Morgan Samuel Editions

Distributed in Canada by Sterling Publishing
c/o Canadian Manda Group, One Atlantic Avenue, Suite 105
Toronto, Ontario, Canada M6K 3E7

Printed and bound by Bath Press Colourbooks, Glasgow

Sterling ISBN 0-8069-0377-5 Trade
0-8069-0670-7 Paperback

CONTENTS

Introduction

Often compared to the blossom of the cherry tree, which sheds its leaves at the moment of its greatest beauty, the samurai — Japan's warrior class for over 1000 years — were considered by many to be the finest expression of the Japanese spirit.

It is difficult for a reader living in the 20th-century industrialised West to understand the values and beliefs of an oriental warrior living in a feudal society. His absolute belief in duty and honour seem naïve from the vantage point of a more cynical age, and the insistence on personal responsibility appears strange to those raised on the notion that individuals are simply products of their environment. It is perhaps this very strangeness that underlies the samurai's enduring fascination. But their appeal extends beyond their ability to excite the imagination; their history is essential reading for anyone interested in the history of Japan.

For centuries, the samurai dominated Japan, controlling much of the economic, religious, intellectual, social and artistic life of the country. It was the samurai government of the Tokugawa family that effectively isolated Japan from foreign influences for two and a half centuries. But when the feudal system that had nurtured the samurai finally collapsed in the middle of the 19th century, and the need for armoured medieval knights vanished, the demands for change and modernisation came from young, forward-thinking samurai.

Japan modernised at an astonishing rate and the warrior became a civil servant or businessman. The traditions and values that had been special to the samurai class were highly respected by many Japanese, and Bushido — the warrior's code — became an expression of national morality.

The samurai coupled skill with weapons with a readiness to die when required that made them formidable warriors. However, to see them as one-dimensional, bloodthirsty fanatics, dedicated only to slaughter and death, would be inaccurate. The ideal samurai were expected to lead austere, disciplined lives, dedicated to their lords and the perfection of the martial arts, and capable of bringing the same finesse to the subtle complexities of the tea ceremony as they would to the removal of an enemy's head on the battlefield.

Confucian ethics underpinned much of samurai thinking, particularly during the Tokugawa period (1598-1868), and the Confucian concept of the shih (gentleman) played an important role in the evolution of the samurai class; the military arts had to be balanced by the acquisition of literary and artistic skills. For example, Miyamoto Musashi (for many, the ultimate master swordsman); though dedicated to the arts of war, was also an expert woodcarver and painter.

The history of the samurai also provides examples of a humanity that defies the bloodthirsty stereotype. While Minamoto Yoshitsune is most famous for his martial exploits in the 12th century, Isabella Bird, the English traveller, discovered a shrine dedicated to him during her journey around Japan in 1878, kept by the Ainu (the indigenous people of the northern island of Hokkaido). Yoshitsune was revered, not as a warrior, but because of the kindness he showed to a people that most Japanese regarded as animals and casually slaughtered for their land.

While the samurai story is a complex history of tremendous bravery and cruelty, tempered on occasion by self-sacrifice and compassion for a defeated enemy, for Western readers the real fascination of the samurai, and

Below: The bold, defiant image of the samurai is captured in this warrior print by Kuniyoshi, the master of the genre.

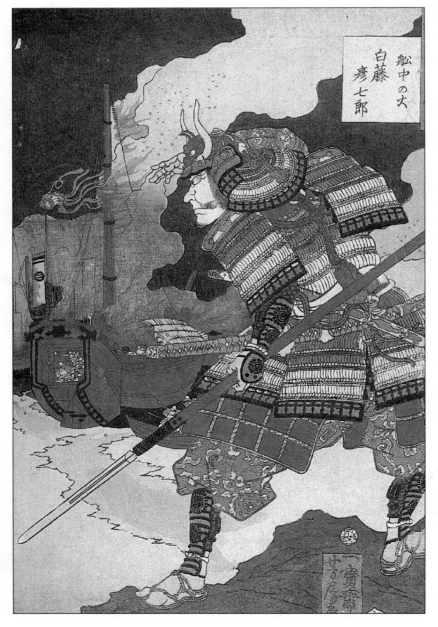

the martial arts associated with them, lies in the fact that they preserved a way of life that vanished in the West with the development of firearms. The carnage inflicted by machine guns, massed artillery and powerful explosives destroyed the Western idea of chivalry; but in the ideal samurai, a man who lived and died according to a code of honour which, in theory at least, was untainted by greed, we can find many qualities to admire.

Those critics who dwell on the violent episodes in the history of the samurai would do well to remember that they lived in harsh times. If they died in combat it was at the hands of another warrior, and not as the result of indiscriminate butchery.

There is a saying in Japanese: 'Umeboshi to tomadachi wa furui hodo yoi', which translates as 'pickled plums and friends; the older the better'. I'm not too sure about the pickled plums but I entirely agree with the rest of the proverb. I would like to thank the following for the generous way they gave of their time, advice and expertise and for being my 'old pickled plums': Graham Noble, Terry O'Neill and 'Fighting Arts International Magazine', Dr David Scott, Julian and Kaoru Mead, Dr Mike Simpson, Alf and Wai-Yin Hatton, Seiretsu Matsui, Ian Garrow for technical assistance, and my wife Sheila for correcting the manuscript and me.

A special word of thanks is due to Mrs Vivienne Ball of the Haltwhistle Public Library, Northumberland, for all her kindness in tracking down some of my more obscure requests for books.

A final word of thanks is due to all my teachers in the martial arts who showed me that the Way of the Samurai is not a thing of the past, but exists as a vital force for personal development and discipline.

Harry Cook
Haltwhistle, 1993

Japanese names follow the normal sequence of family name first, followed by personal name. Instead of trying to follow the confusing habit of changing a person's name at regular intervals, each character is referred to using the name he is most commonly known by.

Above: This map, taken from Utten's 'Atlas Minor' of 1745, depicts Japan at the time of its isolation from the rest of the world, as indicated by the inclusion of a detail of the island of Deshima in Nagasaki Bay, where a few Dutch traders were allowed to operate.

7

The First Warriors

Below: The 'Wedded Rocks' at Futami no Ura are linked by a rope that symbolises the mythological union of the gods Izanagi and Izanami, which created the land of Japan.

The Foundation Myths

According to legend, the Japanese islands were created when the divine couple, Izanagi, 'The Male Who Invites', and Izanami, 'The Female Who Invites', stood on the floating bridge of Heaven and dipped a spear into the ocean below. As the water dripped from the spear's point, it condensed to form the sacred islands of Japan.

To populate these islands, the gods created a large number of divine and semi-divine beings, one of whom claimed direct descent from the Sun Goddess, Amaterasu, and as such held a divine mandate to rule. The mountains, rivers, lakes, trees and other natural manifestations were also divine and regarded as kami, or spirits.

The power of the kami is still affirmed by the native religion of Japan, known as Shinto, or The Way of the Gods, and the mythical account of Japan's origins was subscribed to as recently as the early 20th century. Before

World War II, the importance attached to the cult of the divine emperor meant that scepticism towards the myth of his divine ancestry was considered tantamount to disloyalty. (Even today, some conservative Japanese revere the emperor as a semi-divine being.) However, since World War II, the foundation myths have been superseded by more critical accounts.

The first Japanese

Inevitably, historical explanations of the origins of the Japanese people cannot hope to be so clear-cut as the myths; questions of how the Japanese islands came to be populated, who the first inhabitants were and where they came from, are clouded by uncertainty.

Most historians agree that Japan's population was the product of successive waves of immigration, arriving at different times after the 6th or 7th millennia BC. These were primarily Mongoloid peoples, of various physical and linguistic types, migrating from northern and southeast Asia. Another group, thought to be the ancestors of the Ainu (a Caucasian people, possibly related to the early inhabitants of Siberia), was also present from a very early stage and is generally credited with having been the first Neolithic people to inhabit the islands. Conflicts between the Ainu

THE STRUGGLE FOR LAND

The islands inhabited by the Yayoi, though beautiful, were mainly composed of mountains, with only about 20% of the land fit for farming. With the establishment of agriculture on the islands, this geographical fact took on a new significance that was to have important implications for Japan's development.

As agriculture advanced, terracing of the hillsides released a little more land for growing rice, but productive areas of land remained scarce. The three most fertile areas of Japan are to be found on the main island of Honshu; the largest, the Kanto plain, covers an area of about 12,950 sq km (5000 sq miles). The two others are the Nobi and Kinai plains. The constant struggle for control of these areas provides the background theme of Japanese history.

Another geographical characteristic of the island group would also play an important role in shaping the history of its people. Situated 193 km (120 miles) from the mainland of Asia, the islands were further isolated by difficult ocean currents and summer and winter monsoons. Geographical remoteness precluded continuous contact between Japan and its neighbours, keeping it, on the one hand, relatively safe from invasion, and on the other, free to develop a highly distinctive civilisation.

In time, the Japanese came to appreciate the defence from invasion afforded by their geographical remoteness, and to rejoice in the 'divine' protection the monsoons gave to their islands. Whether divinely managed or merely geographical accident, these circumstances would bear heavily on the development and survival of the samurai.

Below: The key to understanding Japan's history is the struggle for land, illustrated by these carefully and painstakingly terraced paddy fields in the foothills of Mount Fuji.

and the other inhabitants of Japan would characterise much of Japan's later history, but whether or not such conflicts extend back to the earliest times is unclear. Most historians envisage a large degree of fusion between the different immigrant groups.

Archaeological remains, dating from after 4500 BC, show the existence of a hunting and gathering culture, notable for its manufacture of unusually elaborate pottery. This culture (known as the Jomon culture) was disrupted in the 3rd century BC by the arrival of the Yayoi in western Japan. The Yayoi were a more advanced people and are thought to have travelled to Japan from the Korean peninsula. Their excavated remains show that they were familiar with rice cultivation, irrigation, pottery and the use of bronze and iron. Judging by the discovery of Chinese coins and bronze mirrors on the sites of Yayoi settlements, Yayoi culture was subject to continued Chinese influences.

It is impossible to construct an exact picture of the transition between the culture described by Yayoi remains and that of the first recorded Japanese; the myths suggest further waves of immigration from Korea through the southern island of Kyushu. However, we can be sure that by the time of the earliest written records, the inhabitants of Japan were clearly distinct from

their neighbours on the continent, and even exhibited cultural traits, such as ritual purification and extreme respect towards social superiors, that would become recognisable characteristics of later Japanese culture.

Below: A modern reconstruction of a prehistoric Yayoi village in the southern island of Kyushu.

The Divine Warrior

Below right: A statue of the Empress Jingo, who led a Japanese invasion of Korea. She is shown deified as the goddess Nakatsu Hime Zo.

Below: A haniwa of the Kofun period, showing the helmet and armour of the time, and the characteristic straight sword.

From the various creation myths and legends recorded in the 'Kojiki' ('The Record of Ancient Matters' — compiled in 712) and the 'Nihongi' ('Chronicles of Japan' — written eight years later), it is possible to form some ideas about the beginnings of the Japanese state. An heroic figure, Jimmu Tenno — 'The Divine Warrior', who was said to be a direct descendant of Amaterasu, became head of a confederation of various warlike clans. He led his people from Kyushu, where he had maintained links with his Mongolian-Korean ancestral line, moved up the Inland Sea and, after conquering the people of the Kinki region, settled in the area of Yamato. The old records date these events to about 660 BC, a date which is still officially celebrated as the foundation of the Japanese state; but archaeological and other evidence places the migration of Jimmu Tenno and his followers in the 1st century AD. With few written records it is difficult to give accurate dates for the early history of Japan, but behind the myths we can see the gradual establishment and growth of centres of culture, usually at war with all the people around them.

The Yamato state

Among the few records that have survived from this period, the Chinese chronicles known as the Wei records, which date from AD 292, offer tantalising glimpses of early Japan. In these we see the islands' peoples still divided, but apparently making moves towards greater unity under the leadership of a Queen/Priestess called Himiko.

Whether Himiko was an early ruler of the Yamato dynasty is unknown; it seems clear, however, that by the 3rd century AD the political centre of the Japanese people was well established in the Yamato region. The region's inhabitants were tribal and semi-nomadic, divided into extended family groups known as uji, and led by hereditary chieftains who, like Himiko, combined the roles of ruler and priest. Each clan had its own deity, usually an ancestor, and the chieftains derived their power in part from the fact that they maintained the worship of the uji god.

The Yamato state was a loose grouping of uji under the overall leadership of the Yamato clan, which held itself to be of divine origin, making its members the natural rulers of Japan. In later centuries, the divine status accorded to Yamato sovereigns played a crucial political role, preventing other powerful clans from

THE GREAT TOMB BUILDERS

The Wei chronicles record that when Queen Himiko died she was buried with great ceremony under an enormous earthen mound. Between the 2nd and 6th centuries AD, the practice of tomb building spread through much of Japan, from the Yamato plain to north Kyushu. These tombs (or kofun) were astonishing constructions; vast, keyhole-shaped sepulchres, up to 457 m (1500 ft) long and 30.5 m (100 ft) high, they rivalled the Egyptian pyramids in size and, like the tombs of the Pharaohs, were crammed with a wealth of artefacts.

The tombs provide us with important clues as to the nature of early Japanese society. They reflect the presence of a powerful and widespread élite; and the even distribution of the tombs, and uniformity of their contents from region to region, show that the merging of regional cultures was well underway.

The contents of the tombs give us detailed information about the way of life of the people buried within. A myriad of objects, ranging from the symbolic to the everyday, were buried with the dead: jewels, mirrors, pottery, tools and armour. Alongside these, small pottery figures, known as haniwa, have been found in the tombs. Probably intended as grave-markers, their subjects include representations of the people of the time. Dressed in quilted clothing and often armed with straight swords, these figures bear witness to the beginnings of a warrior tradition that would eventually produce the samurai.

Below left: The enormous burial mound of the Emperor Nintoku, near Nara, which is surrounded by a moat.

Below right: The smaller Jieitai Kofun, probably the tomb of an emperor's wife.

replacing the dynasty and forcing them to exercise control of the imperial family indirectly.

During the early centuries of Yamato rule, the Japanese clans were engaged in several military campaigns on the Asian mainland. Legend has it that at one point Yamato troops, led by Empress Jingu, defeated the kingdom of Silla (part of present-day Korea); certainly, during the 5th and 6th centuries, the Japanese gained control of Mimana, a small kingdom in the south-east of Korea. Military expeditions abroad left the fledgling Yamato state prey to internal divisions. In the 5th century, one provincial leader, Iwai, halted an imperial army of over 60,000 troops on its way to Korea; it took a year for the imperial authorities to impose their will. After the 6th century, the Yamato leaders abandoned foreign campaigns and concentrated on developing their authority within Japan.

However, these foreign expeditions had important consequences for Japanese civilisation. The superior technology and culture of China and Korea were imported to enhance the status of the Yamato court: weaving, metal-working, writing, Buddhism and Confucian political philosophy, all made their way to Japan, to be adopted and adapted by the Japanese. The influence of Sino-Korean culture is indicated by the fact that the 'Shojiroku' ('Record of Peerages') written in 815, which recorded the genealogies of the Yamato nobility, showed that one third were of foreign, mainly Korean, origin.

Prince Yamato

Right: Prince Yamato carried out many campaigns against rivals to the imperial house, which have passed into samurai legend. Here he kills a rebel chieftain.

Right: Prince Yamato carried out many campaigns against rivals to the imperial house, which have passed into samurai legend. Here he kills a rebel chieftain.

Below: The Ise Naiku Shrine, established in the 3rd century AD, is dedicated to the Sun Goddess Amaterasu and is the holiest place within the indigenous Japanese religion of Shinto. By a long tradition the shrine is demolished and rebuilt every 20 years in the simple style of plain, unvarnished wood and thatch.

Prince Yamato was said to be the son of the Emperor Keiko, who, according to tradition, was the first emperor to award the title of 'Shogun' ('Barbarian-subduing General') to his generals. He is almost certainly a composite figure, and his adventures are derived, with suitable exaggerations, from the experiences of the warriors sent out to fight the indigenous Ainu and rival clans in the 1st and 2nd centuries AD.

In many ways Prince Yamato could be considered a role model for the samurai, although at this time samurai as such did not exist. While exhibiting a total fearlessness when facing his enemies, Yamato lacked any form of compassion. He killed his elder brother for being late for a meal, so angering his father that he was dispatched to Kyushu to use his martial skills to fight the enemies of the throne.

On the way, he visited his aunt, who was the high priestess at the Great Shrine of Ise — the centre of the worship of the Sun Goddess Amaterasu. He was presented with a sword, taken by the god Susano-o from the tail of a great snake. Known as 'Ame no Murakomo' ('Cloud Cluster'), the sacred sword features prominently in the legends of Prince Yamato.

The legends are numerous but consistently emphasise the qualities of fearlessness and cunning that the samurai demanded of their heroes. Yamato first used the sword when he tricked his way into a rebel leader's banquet disguised as a woman. As his enemy became drowsy and off guard, due to the effects of the food and the wine, Yamato drew his sword and

EARLY WARRIORS

While the men of the clans were farmers, fishermen, weavers or metal workers, they were also warriors. In order to survive and expand, they had to fight the original Caucasian inhabitants whose descendants, the Ainu, may still be found in small numbers in Hokkaido.

From the remains of weapons and armour found in the burial mounds it is possible to picture the equipment used by a warrior of those times. His armour, known as tanko, was made from shaped iron plates. The earliest examples are very similar to the leather and bark armour found in China, using the same method of leather lacing to hold the plates together, but later examples show a distinctive Japanese style, featuring hinges and rivets.

The helmets (kabuto) were made from a curved metal plate, shaped to fit the skull and reinforced with two horizontal metal strips and small iron plates. The sides and the back of the head were protected by U-shaped strips of metal, fastened to the helmet with leather thongs that allowed the protective strips to adapt to the wearer's movements. The body armour, known as do, was constructed from iron plates riveted to a number of horizontal iron bands, which fitted closely to the body. This type of armour was very heavy, and as it was worn by men fighting on foot with swords, spears, bows and arrows, the weight had to be taken on the hips and shoulders, so this type of armour was characterised by a flared shape at the hips. Fastened to the lower edge of the do was a skirt of small, laced metal plates, known as the kusazuri (grass rubbing), designed to protect the upper part of the legs.

The shoulders and upper arms were protected by curved metal plates fastened to the do. The lower arms were protected by a circular piece of plate armour with the back of the hands covered by laced iron scales. In general, all the armour was covered with a coat of lacquer to protect it against the damp, and a pheasant's tail feathers were fastened to the

helmet for decoration. These early warriors were equipped with simple bows made from a single piece of wood, spears with socketed heads similar to earlier Chinese types, and long, straight, single-edged swords made of iron. On average these swords were 1 m (3 ft) long and in many cases were of Chinese manufacture, although it was thought that some examples may have been made by native swordsmiths. Along with other aspects of Chinese civilisation, the Japanese imported large numbers of the small, sturdy, central Asian ponies of the type later used by the Mongols, which allowed them to become more mobile in their fighting tactics.

Below: A terracotta haniwa dressed in an early form of lamellar armour, derived from continental Asiatic styles.

killed two of the rebel chieftains. Later, Yamato was invited to join a stag hunt near Mount Fuji. The hunters tried to kill him by setting the long grass on fire and burning him to death. Once again, he drew his sword and swiftly cut a path to safety through the long grass, in the process renaming the blade 'Kusanagi no tsurugi' ('Grass Cutting Sword').

When Prince Yamato died, poisoned by the same serpent from whose tail his sword had originally been taken, his spirit was transformed into a white bird. The sword Kusanagi was placed in the Atsuta Shrine and

became one of the three sacred regalia of the imperial family, along with a mirror and jewels. Legend tells us that a Chinese priest named Dogyo attempted to steal the blade but it cut itself free and returned to the shrine. Dogyo then wrapped the blade in nine layers of cloth to prevent its escape, and managed to carry the blade away, but the angered spirit of Prince Yamato sent a kami — Sumiyoshi Daimyojin — to recover the blade. In the struggle that followed, the kami kicked the thief to death and then returned the sword to the sacred precincts of the shrine.

SAMURAI ARMOUR

Right: This breastplate is from a well-crafted do, made of embossed solid iron, with lacquered edges.

Below: A fine suit of armour made during the Edo period, but in the style of a typical oyoroi as would have been worn during the 11th century, except for the sashimono (banner) in the form of golden wings at the rear.

The earliest examples of armour worn by Japanese warriors resembled the types found on the Asian mainland. From the 5th century onwards, horses were introduced into Japan and a new type of armour evolved. Made of small metal or leather scales that overlapped and were laced together, it could be worn on horseback, allowing the rider the freedom to load and fire a bow.

Scale, or lamellar, armour had the advantage of being relatively light, which was vital for a mounted archer. Scales and lacing absorbed and dissipated a blow before any serious damage was done to the wearer, and on these early types of armour the only really rigid component was the helmet.

By the time of the wars between the Taira and the Minamoto clans in the 11th and 12th centuries, two basic forms of armour had been developed. The oyoroi (great armour) was worn by high-ranking samurai. Having a square, box-like appearance, this armour featured large shoulder and arm protectors, as

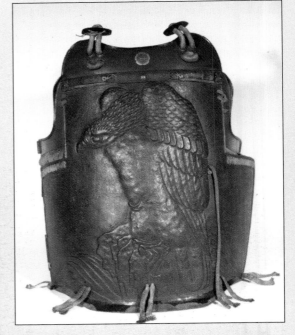

well as a large helmet that included protection for the neck. The haramaki (belly wrap) was a simpler form of armour, worn by low-ranked retainers. This consisted of a body protector made from three or four rows of scales with simple shoulder protectors made from laced rows of scale armour. This type of armour was designed for use on foot and so was lighter than the oyoroi. As the incidence of hand-to-hand combat increased, the mobility and flexibility of the haramaki meant that it became more popular among all levels of the samurai.

With the Mongol invasions in the 13th century, the haramaki was changed by adding better shoulder protection and helmets in order to improve the blend of mobility and protection. The oyoroi was also improved by the addition of greaves to protect the legs, and an armoured skirt or apron was developed to protect the thighs. The neck and face were protected by a gorget and an iron mask, usually resembling a scowling face, and the forearms were protected with mail.

By the 15th century, most high-ranking warriors had abandoned the oyoroi as being impractical for fighting on foot with a sword. They wore an improved version of the haramaki, decorated as befitted their status, along with large helmets made from small plates riveted together. The constant fighting of the period produced a continual demand for effective armour for all ranks of warrior. Simple armour that could be made quickly and cheaply was needed to equip the increasing number of ashigaru (lightly armoured foot-

soldiers) and a new type of armour was made by sewing small metal plates onto a cloth base, with any gaps being protected by mail.

The introduction of firearms, after 1543, meant that armourers needed to develop protection against gunshot and so solid plates began to take precedence over the older lamellar forms. It is not uncommon to see suits of armour that have been tested for their ability to resist musket balls — they often have marks where the musket ball deformed the metal. With the arrival of the Portuguese and other foreigners, the Japanese acquired examples of European armour, some of which were incorporated into suits of armour by Japanese armourers. Tokugawa Ieyasu, who founded the Tokugawa shogunate at the beginning of the 17th century, is said to have worn a suit of armour at the Battle of Sekigahara that included several pieces of European origin.

When the Tokugawa shogunate became established, the need for functional armour largely disappeared. Families of hereditary armourers, such as the Myochin and their related family, the Satome, concentrated on making suits of armour as decorative symbols. They reproduced ancient designs, lavishly

embossed and decorated with lacquer, ivory and precious metals.

The fighting that accompanied the restoration of the emperor, in 1868, provided the last occasion for samurai armour to be worn in battle. Light suits made from hide were worn, but while they were effective in protecting against sword cuts, they could offer little defence against modern rifles and artillery.

Above: A do made entirely from single iron plates, hinged together, shown here opened flat to reveal the construction. Note the holder for a sashimono on the back plate.

Below: A 64-plate iron helmet bowl, showing the holes from which the plates of the shikoro (neckguard) would be suspended.

Prince Shotoku

As the Yamato state grew more complex, the old tribal forms of government were seen to be inefficient and Chinese models of government and administration were adopted. The Yamato sovereigns began to use the title of 'emperor', claiming for themselves all the virtues of the sage rulers of China. To consolidate its control over other clans, the Yamato court also attempted to introduce a more centralised bureaucratic state under the control of the imperial family.

The reforms owed much to the support of the Soga clan. During the 6th century, the Soga emerged as powerful players in the political jostling that surrounded the imperial family. In 587, they defeated the more conservative Mononobe and Nakatomi clans at the Battle of Shigisen; thereafter, the Soga clan dominated the Yamato court. In 592, the head of the clan, Soga Umako, put his niece on the throne and appointed her nephew, Prince Shotoku (574-622), as regent.

Shotoku was half Soga by birth and, with Soga support, he instituted a series of reforms designed to replace the old hereditary system of government with a Chinese system of centralised bureaucracy. The Chinese calendar was adopted; in place of the old hereditary uji ranks, court ranks were given to officials according to their positions in the government; and a set of precepts, known as the '17 Articles Constitution', was issued. Article 12 stated: 'Let not the provincial authorities or the Kuni no Miyakko (the old local nobles) levy exaction on the people.... The officials to whom [the sovereign] gives charge are all his vassals'.

As the frontiers of the Yamato state expanded, local magnates set up their own domains, theoretically as officials of the court. When central authority was at all weak, they tended to pursue their own interests and could only be brought into line by force. So, to enforce the court's authority, the government maintained a standing army.

The Fujiwara family

After Shotoku's death, the Soga clan fell from power. Their despotic rule ended in 645, when Prince Naka (the future Emperor Tenchi — reigned 668-71) took power in a palace revolution organised by Nakatomi Kamatari, head of the Nakatomi clan.

Kamatari (614-69) was given the name of Fujiwara as a sign of imperial favour, the name deriving from wisteria trees found in the valley where he and Prince Naka had met to plan the reform of the government. Fujiwara Kamatari established a line of politicians that would dominate the Japanese court for centuries, repeatedly marrying into the imperial family and controlling the line of succession. Their tenacity was remarkable; between 724 and 1900, 54 of the 76 emperors were born to Fujiwara mothers.

Prince Naka and Kamatari continued the introduction of Chinese methods of government with the Taika Reforms (Great Change Reforms), which began in 645 and continued for several decades. All land was declared to belong to the emperor. The intention was to redistribute land to some extent; every male over five years old was to be given about half an acre of land: every female, a little less. The great landowners would remain in control of their own land, but as government appointees. They were given court rank and titles, and the authority to administer the land in the emperor's name, for which they were to be paid according to their rank. Taxation was due to the central government in the form of

THE ARRIVAL OF BUDDHISM

Buddhism was first brought to Japan in the early 6th century by travellers from Korea. The new religion found powerful patrons in the Soga clan, and after their victory at the Battle of Shigisen, it became accepted at the imperial court. Already over 800 years old by this time, Buddhism became the vehicle for a wholesale transfer of Chinese civilisation into Japan.

Inevitably, the new religion aroused some hostility on behalf of Japan's indigenous cults, and the struggle between the Buddhist Soga and the Mononobe and Nakatomi clans can be seen in this light (the Nakatomi were traditionally priests of the Shinto cults). However, the form of Buddhism that reached Japan was tolerant of other religions, and relations between the old and new religions soon settled into peaceful co-existence. At first, Buddhism was confined to the court, where it was welcomed as a rich source of new magical formulae. Its most radical impact in the early years was aesthetic: the religion's long history had produced a sophistication of thought and artistic tradition that the court found irresistible, and it inspired a flowering of Chinese-style arts in Japan.

Over the centuries, Buddhism's influence filtered down into the rest of Japanese society. Alongside Confucianism, which had arrived in Japan a few years earlier, it became the inspiration for many important features of Japanese culture. It brought an end to tomb burials, which were replaced by cremation; and meat, other than fish, became a rarity in the Japanese diet. Moreover, Buddhist ideas of the impermanence of life and the non-existence of self became an important influence on the development of samurai traditions of self-sacrifice and the ethicacy of suicide.

Below:
A relief carving of a Buddha hewn out of a natural rock face, typical in style of many thousands of representations of the founder of the newly introduced religion.

rice, labour and military service. These policies were continued by successive emperors, and a centralised form of government gradually became established.

The Taiho (Great Treasure) law codes of 702 established the Great Council of State as the supreme administrative body of government. This was presided over by the Chancellor, who was assisted by a Minister of the Left and a Minister of the Right, who in turn oversaw the functions of eight government ministries.

While the Japanese faithfully copied the outer forms of Chinese government, they failed to adopt the Chinese example of selecting officials according to their scholarship and ability. The new forms of government in Japan were staffed by the old aristocracy, so perpetuating the traditional hereditary system.

New Capitals

Centralised government required a base and in 710 the first permanent capital was established at the northern end of the small Nara (also called Yamato) plain. Originally called Heijo, it is better known as Nara, and the years from 710 to 784 are known as the Nara period.

The plan of the city was based on that of the Chinese city of Ch'ang-an, the capital of the T'ang dynasty. The main streets were laid out on a grid system with the imperial palace and associated buildings at the north end. Large Buddhist temples were built, and native sects of Japanese Buddhism appeared. The patronage of Buddhism by the imperial family cost the state a lot of money; at one point 116 priests were attached to the court as exorcists and one of the temples owned over 2023 hectares (5000 acres) of the best land, without paying any tax to the government.

The Council of State, reacting to the threat that the growing financial and political power of Buddhism represented to their authority, arranged matters so that in 781 a strong emperor — Emperor Kammu — came to the throne. In 784, the capital was moved to Nagaoka, but this site was not acceptable due to it being haunted by the spirit of a murdered official. After consulting experts in the Chinese art of feng-shui (geomancy: literally 'wind and water', the Chinese art of divination), a new capital was established at Kyoto. Given the name of Heian Kyo, the Capital of Eternal Tranquillity, the new city was built according to the Chinese grid design used in Ch'ang-an and at Nara.

The central government depended on the

WARS AGAINST THE AINU

As the government and aristocracy of the Japanese state settled into a life of refinement and elegance, the farmers on the frontiers lived a very different life. Forced to fight the Emishi (or barbarians, as the Ainu were also known) for every inch of land, the government had to spend huge amounts of money and resources to pay for troops to protect the frontiers from raids mounted by the Ainu, sometimes in league with renegade Japanese, unwilling to accept central government control.

In 776, a rebellion broke out in the north and the town of Taga, near the modern city of Sendai, was attacked. Government troops, raised from the central rather than the frontier regions, proved useless in fighting the Ainu; they were untrained in the use of weapons and were commanded by men who were more ornamental than functional, having no experience of warfare and being unskilled in fighting. They had no answer to the tactics favoured by the Ainu who, according to the historian George Sansom, 'gathered together like ants, but dispersed like birds'. The Ainu's mobility and general fighting skill meant that, at best, the government forces could contain them but could not defeat them.

Clearly a new solution was necessary, and the government ordered the formation of local defence forces, made up of skilled young men drawn from the families of district chiefs. Exempted from taxation in kind or in labour, these groups were expected to police and protect their local regions. Responsibility for defence was transferred from provincial governors and centrally controlled troops to bands of men recruited on a hereditary basis from the households of local landowners. It is here that we can see the beginnings of the samurai class. Although these provincial warrior bands were despised by the courtiers in Kyoto, within four centuries they had relegated the imperial court to a ceremonial role, becoming the only real power in the land.

Left: A painted scroll depicting the characteristically hairy appearance of the Ainu, the aboriginal inhabitants of Japan, who fought the incoming settlers.

wealth it acquired through taxation. However, many of the larger landowners managed to obtain tax exemption, as did many religious institutions. They became the patrons of others, extending their freedom from taxation for the payment of a fee.

This system, known as kishin, meant that certain families, most notably the Fujiwara, became very wealthy. This, combined with the Fujiwara's continuous domination of the court, resulted in the concentration of power and wealth in the hands of a small number of families at the expense of the state. The large

manors and estates, known as shoen, gradually drained away the tax revenue, so weakening the authority and power of the central government and paving the way for a shift of power from central government to the large landowners.

Newly cultivated land in the north and the east was exempted from taxation as a means of repaying the costs incurred by the landowners. The manors became very powerful and, as ownership became hereditary, the interests and wishes of the landowners replaced the dictates of government policy.

The First Shoguns

Right: An Ainu archer as imagined by a European artist in 1800 from descriptions given to him by travellers who must have had some brief contact with Japan's most northerly territories.

In 784, Otomo Yakamochi was given the rank of 'Seito Shogun' ('General for Subduing the East'). His task was to defeat the Ainu and their renegade Japanese allies, but his defensive tactics and passive approach had little or no effect. Otomo Yakamochi is notable for one thing; he was one of the first men to be given the title of shogun, a rank that most of the samurai leaders valued for over 1000 years.

Otomo Yakamochi died in 786, and three years later Ki no Kosami was appointed to lead the imperial troops. He was given command of 52,000 cavalry and foot soldiers and began a campaign against the Ainu. He wrote that in one engagement he lost '25 killed, 245 wounded by arrows, 1316 thrown into the river and drowned'. Around 1000 more were captured, stripped of their armour and thrown in the river. In reply, the Japanese took less than 100 Ainu heads as trophies.

Below: A modern statue of a warrior of between AD 500 and 700, wearing the solid plate tanko style of armour that preceded lamellar forms.

The Emperor Kammu was furious and wrote that 'our generals... complain of the difficulties of transport, but the truth is that they are incompetent cowards'. Ki no Kosami and his generals were put on trial and sentenced to death, but in fact Kosami was pardoned and his senior officers were deprived of military and court rank. They were all men of high social standing, and had been appointed because of patronage and privilege, a system that almost guaranteed failure in battle against experienced and determined opponents.

A new approach

The government realised that to deal with the threat of the Ainu a more determined spirit was needed. In the spring of 790, a levy was enforced on all the provinces and even officials and aristocrats were made to contribute.

Large quantities of rice and other foodstuffs were collected; 20,000 suits of leather armour were requisitioned, along with 3000 suits of iron armour, and around 34,500 arrows were made. Because, in the past, many wealthy and able-bodied people had evaded military service and the requisition of essential supplies, the Council of State ordered a survey to be made of those able to furnish extra supplies, encompassing all ranks and classes.

The commanders of the new forces were chosen in 791, but due to the extensive preparations the new shogun was not appointed until 794. He was Otomo Otomaro, a member of a distinguished aristocratic family who were the hereditary guards of the emperor.

LIFE IN KYOTO

As the frontier areas became stronger and more independent, the centre at Kyoto became progressively more introverted and weak. Courtiers spent their time on writing poetry, calligraphy contests and amorous pursuits, living a refined, sensitive life far removed from the everyday world outside the court. The stoic virtues of the samurai were nowhere to be found.

The exquisite court culture of Heian Kyoto produced a remarkable artistic heritage, particularly in literature. Writers such as Sei Shonagon and Murasaki Shikibu, both female members of the court, wrote of the ideal courtier, a man who would shed tears at the sight of the sun setting or at the thought of leaving his mistress.

For warriors, however, they reserved a more disdainful tone. To the Kyoto aristocracy (the yoki hito, or persons of quality) the men raised on the frontier were simply crude, boorish provincials, unworthy of serious consideration; events outside the court were of little importance; and the mass of the people (the tadabito, or mere persons) had no place in the life of the governing élite.

Real power shifted to the east and the court in Kyoto gradually became nothing more than a faded symbol of imperial strength. The situation had deteriorated so much that, by the year 1000, the imperial police could no longer maintain order in the city or control the attacks of robbers in the surrounding countryside.

By 1040, the situation had become so desperate that the imperial palace was attacked by thieves who stole some of Emperor Gosozaku's clothing. Perhaps this is not so surprising as the man appointed to command the city police in 1025 was aged 17 and had been selected for his good looks, high court rank and wealth. The centre was crumbling and unable to control events. A new force was needed to step in to the political vacuum and take control. That force was the samurai.

Below: Prince Genji practises his calligraphy in an illustration to Lady Murasaki Shikibu's novel, 'The Tale of Genji'. One of the world's oldest novels, it idealises the life and intrigues of the Kyoto court.

Learning from their past mistakes, the government appointed a competent deputy commander, Sakanouye no Tamura Maro. The subsequent success of the forces under his command attests to his military skills.

Sakanouye built and garrisoned strong-holds in the north at Izawa and Shiba, and from these bases gradually subdued the Ainu and their allies. The frontier lands were pacified by building a chain of frontier forts and by settling farmers on the new lands to act as a frontier guard. The cost of building two new capitals and fighting wars against the Ainu severely depleted the imperial treasury. In 805, a Fujiwara minister sent a memorandum to the throne in which he complained that 'at present the state is suffering from two things: building and warfare'. These costs, coupled with the widespread tax evasion practised by large estates and religious bodies, meant that the heart of the state became progressively weaker and poorer as the frontiers expanded. The new lands, which should have resulted in an increase of revenue for the state, were also largely tax exempt, so increasing the wealth and power of landowners far from Kyoto.

The Emergence of the Samurai

Founding the Clans

Below: A statue of a Deva King, dressed in contemporary Chinese armour, which shows clearly the influence that came to Japan from the continent.

As the imperial family grew larger, it became necessary to limit the number of princes and other royal ranks. The Taiho Law Code of AD 702 included a provision that descendants of emperors in the sixth generation were to be reduced from the rank of prince, given a family name and expected to live independent lives.

Many of the dispossessed nobles duly left the Fujiwara dominated court at Kyoto and made their way to the frontier regions, where land, status and power could be obtained by those with the necessary intelligence and strength.

The nobles' court ranks stood them in good stead, for although the provincial landowners rejected political control from Kyoto, there was still a lingering respect for the prestige of the Kyoto court. Many of the most powerful landowners were proud to trace their origins to offshoots of the imperial line or to aristocratic families of the court at Kyoto.

As the power and wealth of the central government declined, local government officials increasingly lacked the means to enforce the law. New sources of authority were needed in the localities and the owners of the large estates managed to secure the right to provide their own security by maintaining private armies. This led to an increase in violent confrontations between local groups over land or political offices.

Initially, these groups of armed retainers were composed of members of related families, but gradually non-related individuals, known as kenin (housemen), were recruited. The class of provincial warriors that emerged between the 9th and 12th centuries was known as bushi (warriors) or samurai (knights/retainers).

Drawn from a mixture of the descendants of the old clan aristocracy and the minor branches of the Kyoto nobility, the samurai's primary obligation was to his lord and his domain, and not to any form of central government. A feudal-like system evolved, in which the warrior gave unqualified loyalty to his lord in return for land rights, status and protection.

The battle for power

It has been said that the political history of the Heian period (794-1184) is simply a record of the fortunes of three clans; the Taira, the Minamoto and the Fujiwara.

By long tradition, the ancient Fujiwara clan was closely identified with the imperial family and, although they owned large estates and wielded tremendous power, they lacked the military means to protect themselves. The Fujiwara's real power was eclipsed when the authority of the imperial family declined. The Minamoto were also descended from various imperial offspring, with each branch including the name of the emperor from which it claimed descent. In general, the

Left: The Heian Shrine was built during the last century to commemorate the 1000th anniversary of the foundation of Kyoto as the capital city. It is a replica of the original imperial palace in Kyoto.

Minamoto supported the policies of the Fujiwara family, so much so that Minamoto Yorimitsu and Minamoto Yorinobu became known as the 'running dogs' of the Fujiwara clan.

The Taira were founded by Taira Takamochi, a grandson of Emperor Kammu (737-806) who had been appointed governor of Hitachi in the east of Japan. Over the years, the descendants of Takamochi increased the power and wealth of their clan to the point where they felt they could challenge the imperial government.

Masakado's revolt

The political tensions produced by declining imperial authority came to a head in 935, when Taira Masakado, a powerful landowner in the east, rose in revolt against Kyoto and proclaimed himself 'the New Emperor'.

Masakado was a formidable figure. His Taira pedigree was coupled with a ruthless determination to expand his territory, regardless of the cost to his neighbours and relations. In the 'Konjaku Monogatari' ('Tales of Now It Is A Long Time Ago'), a military chronicle compiled in about 1080, we are told that this violent man 'made battle his way of life' and that he 'invariably dealt with any matter by having recourse to battle. He burned down many men's houses and he took many men's lives'.

At first, Masakado argued with his uncle, Yoshikane, about some disputed rice fields. He was prepared to go to war over the land but his uncle, being a devout Buddhist, refused to fight. Masakado then acquired more land through pillage, until called to Kyoto to explain his behaviour. After examining his actions, the imperial authorities decided that he had done no wrong and he was allowed to return home.

True to his nature, Masakado wasted no time in resuming his pursuit of power, quarrelling with his uncles, Yoshikane and Yoshimasa, as well as two Minamoto landowners, Mamoru and Tasuku, and eventually open warfare broke out. He also earned the enmity of his cousin, Taira Sadamori, after killing Sadamori's father, Kunika, in 935.

As Masakado increased his enemies, he also managed to attract other disaffected warriors to his side. Prince Okiyo, the acting governor of Musashi (a position that he had seized by force), attacked the government-appointed agents in the region and formed an alliance with Masakado.

Although Minamoto Tsunemoto reported these events to the throne in 939, nothing was done to check Masakado's belligerence; in fact, the government in Kyoto gave tacit approval for the actions of Masakado and his allies. The situation escalated and Fujiwara Haruaki, in the province of Hitachi, rose in revolt, drove out the governor, Fujiwara Korechika, and joined Masakado's forces

Right: The hero Fujiwara (or Tawara) Hidesato, who defeated Taira Masakado, the self-styled 'New Emperor'.

Below: The death of Masakado, flung from his horse by an arrow from the army of Fujiwara Hidesato.

The New Emperor

As the ranks of Masakado's allies grew larger, so too did his arrogance. Confident that his forces were strong enough, Masakado next expanded into the neighbouring provinces and, after seizing the seals and keys of office from the government-appointed officials, he began to establish his own court and government.

Having set himself up in opposition to the imperial government, Masakado needed to legitimise his own claim to the throne. So he was delighted when an oracle in a trance declared that he had a message from the God of War, Hachiman, which confirmed Masakado's right to the throne. 'We confer Our Imperial Rank on Our Favoured Child, Taira no Masakado', the message went. 'Quickly welcome him reverently with music'. With his claim to be the New Emperor so

conveniently affirmed, Masakado proceeded to consolidate his gains. A warning note was sounded by his younger brother, Masahira, who reminded him, 'To reach the position of emperor is something conferred by Heaven. You had better meditate well on this'.

The New Emperor replied, 'The Way of the Bow and Arrow is enough for me. In these times one is sovereign because one overcomes. Why should I hold back?'.

'Kyusen no Michi', or The Way of the Bow and Arrow, means the way of life adopted by the élite samurai. To Masakado, this martial philosophy (known to later generations as Bushido, or The Way of the Warrior) was the source from which his strength flowed.

The fall of Masakado

The period of Masakado's ascendancy was a brief one. Faced with the prospect of a powerful New Emperor, Masakado's enemies united against him, stating: 'We should rescue the Noble Houses from shame; we should fight him without regard for our lives'. Faced with superior forces, Masakado was forced onto the defensive and his armies were gradually whittled away. His home and the homes of his leading supporters were burned by his cousin Sadamori, and the fortunes of the New Emperor went into decline.

The 'Konjaku Monogatari' described his fate: 'The New Emperor then had only some 400 warriors because the 8000 ... who always followed him were not yet mustered. So he prepared a position on the North Mountain of Sashima and awaited the enemy. Sadamori, Hidesato and their men came in pursuit and engaged in battle. At first, the New Emperor had the advantage and threw back the warriors of Sadamori, Hidesato and their party, but these men in their turn won the

THE SAMURAI ASCENDANT

Masakado's rebellion clearly showed that at least some of the warrior class were aware of their power and were prepared to use it to achieve their ambitions. The government adopted a policy of using the warriors of one samurai clan to limit the expansionist tendencies of others, a policy which, though expedient, gave the samurai a central role in Japanese politics.

From the 10th century onwards, strong samurai leaders began to exert an increasing influence over the direction of Japanese history. Real imperial government gradually became impossible due to the constant power struggles between Fujiwara regents, titular emperors, retired emperors, powerful ministers and provincial landlords. In reality, no one outside the court took any notice of imperial edicts unless it suited their own interests, and the only effective form of government in the provinces became that of the samurai clans, who ruled themselves according to their own clan laws.

The Fujiwara attempted to limit the influence of the samurai by using the strengths of the rival clans to neutralise one another, a policy that could only be effective as long as one clan did not dominate the others. If one clan were to emerge in a dominant position, the weakness at the centre of the imperial system would be exposed for all to see, and the imperial family and their Fujiwara regents would be brushed aside and given, at best, a symbolic role to play.

Below: This section from a painted scroll shows a battle between rival samurai. Note the use of naginata, the wooden shields, and a hooked rake.

advantage. They fought together without begrudging their lives.

'When the New Emperor himself engaged in battle and sped on his swift horse, the Punishment of Heaven was openly revealed; his horse no longer ran, his hand lost its skill, and finally, struck by an arrow, he died in the midst of the plain. Sadamori, Hidesato and their group rejoiced at this and ordered a fierce warrior to cut off his head.

They sent it up to the capital, accompanied by an official letter from the province of Shimotsuke'.

The court, quite naturally, was relieved to hear of Masakado's death and instantly sent out orders to hunt down and kill all of Masakado's brothers, dependents and followers. The men who had so successfully led the forces against Masakado were rewarded with official positions and court ranks.

THE WAY OF THE WARRIOR

Masakado's high regard for The Way of the Bow and Arrow was characteristic of the samurai class throughout its history. With the assumption of power by the Tokugawa in the 17th century, Japan entered an extended period of peace, during which some samurai writers spent their time detailing the behaviour of the ideal samurai. The code of values they described became known as Bushido, or The Way of the Warrior.

This code dominated all aspects of the samurai's social and personal relationships. The term 'bu' means martial and is derived from Chinese, where the character is read as 'wu'. It is mentioned in a poem, 'Battle', by the poet Ch'u Yuan (332-295 BC). Although Ch'u Yuan was describing the virtues of Chinese warriors, the poem can be interpreted as a guide to the essence of Bushido:

Below: A samurai archer, symbolic of 'The Way of Horse and Bow', the code of chivalry that preceded the better known Bushido.

'We grasp our battle-spears: we don our
    breast-plates of hide.
The axles of our chariots touch: our short
    swords meet.
Standards obscure the sun: the foe roll up
    like clouds.
Arrows fall thick: the warriors press
    forward.
They menace our ranks: they break our line.
The left-hand trace horse is dead: the one
    on the right is smitten.
The fallen horses block our wheels: they
    impede the yoke-horses!
They grasp their jade drum-sticks: they
    beat the sounding drums.
Heaven decrees their fall: the dread Powers
    are angry.
The warriors are all dead: they lie on the
    moor-field.
They issued but shall not enter: they went
    but shall not return.
The plains are flat and wide: the way home
    is long.
Their swords lie beside them: their black
    bows, in their hand.
Though their limbs were torn, their hearts
    could not be repressed.
They were more than brave: they were
    inspired by the spirit of Wu.
Steadfast to the end, they could not be
    daunted.
Their bodies were stricken, but their souls
    have taken Immortality.
Captains among the ghosts, heroes among the
    dead'.

One of the earliest mentions of a specific warrior code is to be found in the 'Konjaku Monogatari', in which Tachibana Norimitsu is complimented on his fidelity to the Kyusen no Michi, or The Way of the Bow and Arrow, also known as Kyuba no Michi, or The Way of the Bow and Horse (the references to archery and horses are a reminder that Japanese warriors originally fought as horse archers).

Freedom from fear

The 'Hagakure' ('The Hidden Leaves', written by Yamamoto Tsunemoto in 1716) begins with the famous line that Bushido is found in death. This may at first appear to be an invitation to suicide, but it actually means that the samurai is expected to transcend his fear of death so that he may serve his lord faithfully and die well if required.

Yagyu Munenori, the famous master of the sword and instructor to the Tokugawa shogun, Iemitsu, was once approached by a samurai who asked to be accepted as a student. Munenori was

puzzled as he felt the man facing him to be a skilled swordsman, and so he asked the samurai to tell him what style he belonged to and the name of his teacher. The samurai replied that he had never studied swordsmanship. Munenori responded sharply, insisting that the man must have already mastered the sword.

Faced with the warrior's persistent denials, Munenori asked him if he had mastered anything. The man paused for a moment and then answered: 'When I was a child I realised that a samurai should never fear death, and from that time I have made an effort to deal with that problem. Now I have no fear of death'.

Munenori smiled and said: 'The essence of the art of the sword is to be free of the fear of death. Of all my students, no one has really grasped this. You do not need to train; you have already mastered the art'.

Under the Tokugawa, the role of the samurai changed and so did their perception of Bushido. Yamaga Soko stressed the Confucian virtue of duty and saw the samurai as a role model for society; by practising Bushido, the samurai acquires virtue that benefits everyone. Daidoji Yuzan's work 'Budo Shoshinshu' refers to the need for a samurai to balance his martial studies with more peaceful accomplishments, such as the tea ceremony or verse-making.

The need to divert the energies of the samurai away from a single-minded devotion to war, and absorb them into the structure of the peaceful Tokugawa state, changed the nature of Bushido. Through hard spiritual training, known as 'seishin tanren', it was believed that 'satsujin no ken' ('the sword that kills'), would become 'katsujin no ken' ('the sword that gives life'). This type of Bushido is still followed by practitioners of the martial arts.

Above: The encounter between the armies of Sanada Yukimura (on the left), commander of the Osaka garrison, and Honda Tadatomo, from the Tokugawa force, during the 'Summer Campaign' of the Siege of Osaka Castle in 1615. Yukimura is one of the later exemplars of Bushido values on the battlefield, being brave and resolute, and dying a hero's death.

Left: A warrior, identified as belonging to the family of Satomi, gives a good account of himself against three opponents in a fine demonstration of the martial values of Bushido.

27

Wars and Insurrections

Below: A suit of armour from the Itsukushima Shrine on the island of Miyajima, which is an excellent example of an 11th-century oyoroi. Very few genuine specimens such as this have survived.

In the north of Honshu, government power was represented by an appointed governor and also by a specially appointed superintendent, whose function was to oversee and control the subjugated Ainu, known at this time by the derogatory name of Fushu (captives).

This office had become the exclusive preserve of the Abe family, a wealthy and powerful clan that had increasingly refused to accept government control. In 1050, the government decided that the troublesome Abe should be taxed and their authority reduced, and so Minamoto Yoriyoshi was appointed to enforce the government's authority and to limit the actions of Abe Yoritoki, the head of the clan.

The ensuing struggle between the Abe clan and the Minamoto and their Fujiwara allies is known as the 'Early Nine Years' War'. Abe Yoritoki was killed by an archer in 1057, but his son, Sadato, took command of his family's forces and continued the struggle to protect his clan's domains.

Towards the end of 1057, Sadato placed 4000 warriors in a strong defensive position at Kawasaki, where they waited to be attacked by the smaller Minamoto forces of 1800 men, led by Yoriyoshi and his eldest son, Yoshiie. The attack failed and, as the Minamoto forces withdrew, Abe Sadato led his men in a counter attack, under the cover of a tremendous blizzard.

Although forced to withdraw, a number of the Minamoto samurai distinguished themselves by their bravery when fighting a rearguard action. One in particular, Minamoto Yoshiie (1041-1103), earned the acclaim of being known as 'Hachiman Taro', the first-born son of the God of War.

The 'Konjaku Monogatari' is effusive in its praise for this exemplary sumarai leader. It says of him that he 'excelled other men in feats of daring. No arrow that he fired was wasted, but enemy arrows fired against him were all to no avail. The barbarians (Sadato's Ainu troops) yielded and ran before him, and there was none bold enough to face him'.

The defeat of the Abe

Stung by this defeat, the Minamoto called upon their allies, the Kiyowara, who sent a large number of troops, led by Kiyowara Mitsunori and his younger brother, Takenori.

In 1062, Yoriyoshi returned to the war in command of 10,000 warriors. This time his efforts yielded far greater success. Although Abe Sadato resisted fiercely from his stockade at Kuriyagawa, with young boys, old men and women fighting side by side with the warriors of their clan against the Minamoto and their allies, the vastly outnumbered Abe were defeated in battle and their strongholds destroyed by fire.

Fujiwara Tsunekiyo, one of Sadato's allies, was captured during the campaign. He had formerly been one of Yoriyoshi's retainers, but was related to Sadato by marriage and had changed sides during the war, taking 800 of his own warriors to strengthen Sadato's forces.

Yoriyoshi was determined to punish his disloyalty and to make him an example to others. He had Tsunekiyo brought before him in order to denouce him. 'You are a hereditary retainer of mine', he said, 'but you recently treated me with contempt and made light of the imperial prestige and authority, and so your offence is most grave'.

十八番弓

Left: Minamoto Yoshiie was one of the most celebrated of the early samurai leaders. He is shown in this portrait scroll dressed in the typical armour of the period.

Below: An illustration from the 'Gunyoki' showing the correct way of presenting an enemy's severed head. Note the spiked board, the identifying label bearing the names of the victor and his victim, and the carefully delineated positions of the hands.

Yoriyoshi's revenge

Instead of using a sharp blade to decapitate Tsunekiyo with a single blow, Yoriyoshi selected a blunt sword and hacked off Tsunekiyo's head in order to cruelly prolong his suffering.

Sadato's demise is described at length in the 'Konjaku Monogatari': 'Sadato drew his sword and cut at the troops, but they stabbed him with their spears. Then they put him on a big shield and carried him into the presence of the governor. Sadato's height was more than 6 ft, and he was 7 ft, 5 inches around the waist; he was imposing in figure and white of skin. He was 44 years old. The governor looked at him and was well pleased, and cut off his head... Sadato had a thirteen-year-old son called Chiyo Doji, a handsome boy; coming out of the palisade, he had fought well. The governor took pity on him and thought to spare him, but Takenori put a stop to this and had his head cut off.

'At the time the palisade fell, Sadato's wife, holding a three-year-old child, said to her husband, "My lord, you are about to be killed. I cannot live alone, and so I will die while you watch". At this, she threw herself into the deep river while still holding the child'.

The severed heads of Sadato, Shigeto (Sadato's brother) and Tsunekiyo were sent to the capital. In a sad postscript to the story, it is said that the men carrying the boxes containing the heads were ordered to prepare the heads for public display by washing and combing the topknots. They were ex-retainers of Sadato who had surrendered, and they complained that there were no combs to prepare the heads properly. They were told to use their own combs and, with tears in their eyes, they complied with the order.

On February 16, 1063, the rebels' heads were stuck on spears, paraded through the streets of Kyoto and left on public display outside the West Jail.

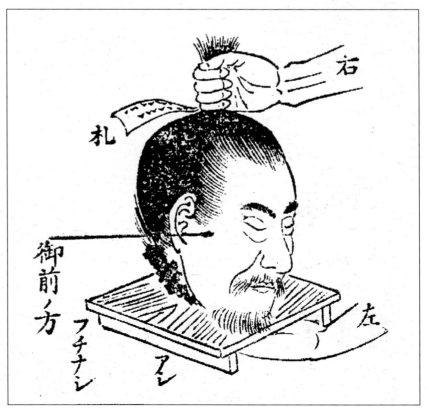

御前ノ方　フチナレ　札　右　左　シレ

Later Three Years' War

During the fighting against the Abe, Yoshiie had promised Hachiman, the God of War, that if he was victorious he would establish a shrine in his honour. True to his promise, he broke his journey to Kyoto at Tsurugaoka, now part of Kamakura, where he built the Tsurugaoka Hachiman shrine in 1063.

Yoshiie was rewarded for his success against the Abe by promotion to the Junior Fifth Rank, Lower Grade. He was also made governor of Dewa, while his father Yoriyoshi was promoted to Senior Fourth Rank and made governor of Iyo. The Kiyowara family were rewarded for their help to the Minamoto during the Early Nine Years' War by being given authority in northern Honshu. History repeated itself and, like the Abe family, the Kiyowara abused their position by increasing their own strength at the expense of the central government. Once again, Minamoto Yoshiie took the field to re-establish government control in the region.

Below: The Tsurugaoka Hachiman Shrine at Kamakura was particularly honoured by the Minamoto clan, although it is best known for certain tragic events associated with them.

The Later Three Years' War was focused around a siege of the Kiyowara's stronghold at Kanezawa. As Minamoto Yoshiie led his forces to confront the Kiyowara samurai, he avoided an ambush by observing a flock of wild geese rising from the woods where the enemy troops lay in wait. Evidently, Yoshiie had studied the Chinese military classic 'The Art of War' by Sun Tzu (Sonshi in Japanese), written during the period of the Warring States (476-221 BC), in which the warning is given that: 'birds rising in flight is a sign that the enemy is lying in ambush; when the wild animals are startled and flee, he is trying to take you unaware'.

'The Art of War'

Sun Tzu's work on military methods was brought to Japan at an early date, possibly in the 6th century. The 'Nihon Genzaisho Mokuroku' ('A Catalogue of Books Existing in Japan'), written by Fujiwara-no-Sukeyo in 891, lists six different editions of Sun Tzu's work. The ideas and concepts contained in this book saturated

samurai thinking and had a powerful and continuous influence on their development. ('The Art of War' is still read by military strategists worldwide and even, reputedly, by Japanese businessmen anxious to secure victory in their commercial war against foreign and domestic competition.)

During the siege of Kanezawa, the defenders resisted bravely and the Minamoto warriors were repulsed time after time. To encourage his men, Yoshiie set aside seats near to his own for those who fought bravely and acts of heroism were lavishly praised.

At this time, the samurai did not fight in disciplined groups under the command of senior officers; they fought individually, as mounted archers, in order to catch the eye of their commanders and so earn rank and land as rewards for their courage. The key weapon of the samurai was the bow and arrow. Although swords were used to remove heads or in close-quarter skirmishes, the sword had not yet become the dominant weapon in the samurai's arsenal. The usual tactic in samurai combat at this time was to dash straight at the enemy on horseback and engage a worthy opponent in an archery duel.

Tactics and strategy, while not ignored by the samurai, were not considered as valuable as fighting spirit, skill and absolute loyalty. During the fighting at Kanezawa, a 16-year-old

samurai, Gongoro Kagemasa, was shot in the eye by an arrow, but he calmly returned fire and killed his attacker. Later, one of his comrades, Miura Tametsugu, tried to remove the arrow by putting his foot on the wounded man's face and pulling on the arrow shaft, but Gongoro objected in the strongest terms; not to the pain but to the fact that someone had dared to stand on his face, an insult which might lead to a fight to the death.

The victorious go unrewarded

The war came to an end when the Minamoto samurai made a final all-out attack and destroyed the Kiyowara stronghold. Taking large numbers of heads as proof of his victory, Yoshiie expected to be rewarded by the government for his service.

In this he was disappointed; the government refused to reward him stating that as he had not been appointed shogun, he had no claims to any sort of official recognition or reward. Disgusted with this reception, he abandoned the heads of his enemies in a ditch and rewarded his men from his own lands.

This short-sighted action by the court was to have serious repercussions; instead of fighting in the name of the court, the tendency of the samurai to fight in their own interests was encouraged and the pretence of imperial authority was finally abandoned.

Above: Minamoto Yoshiie, flying the white banner of the Minamoto family, sets out to fight in the Later Three Years' War.

WATCHING THE ENEMY

Right: Kumawaka, whose daring escape after an assassination was the prototype for the classic ninja activities.
Below: An ambush is carried out on a lone samurai by a group concealed in a wood. A samurai trained in zanshin would learn to look for suspicious movements in undergrowth, and be prepared.

One of the most highly-prized skills among the samurai was zanshin (alertness). When training with the sword — or with any other weapon — the warrior was taught to be aware of his surroundings and his opponent, so that he was always prepared for a surprise attack.

Even when executing a bow in training, the eyes were always kept on the opponent. This tradition has been preserved by modern practitioners of the martial arts. Today's pupils of classical ken-jutsu, studying under a sensei (teacher) of the classical style of Yagyu Shinkage Ryu, sometimes spend their first lesson learning how to bow correctly. This apparently simple task is made difficult because, as pupils lower their heads to the floor, they are struck hard by a

wooden sword. This is continued until the pupil manages to bow and avoid being hit, having therefore learned the vital importance of zanshin.

When learning swordsmanship, some individuals develop their awareness to such a high level that they seem to have supernatural skills. Kurosawa's film 'The Seven Samurai' features a fine example of this in a scene dealing with the selection of the samurai. As they walk through a doorway, prospective warriors are attacked by a youth with a stick; some are hit on the head and neck, others manage to disarm the attacker, but the really superior swordsmen stop and refuse to go through the door as they sense that something is wrong.

Sensing danger

Yagyu Munenori (1571-1646) is remembered for his highly developed sense of zanshin. One day, while walking with an attendant to look at the cherry blossom in his garden, he began to look around, as if searching for someone. Apart from the young attendant he was alone and as he walked back to his house he was obviously deep in thought and seemed greatly troubled.

Worried by his expression, Munenori's servants asked if he was feeling ill. He replied that he had just experienced something strange that he could not understand. Due to his extensive experience he was able to sense the thoughts and emotions of anyone who faced him with the sword, and while in the garden he had sensed extreme danger, yet he could see no enemies. The attendant stepped forward and begged his forgiveness. He told Yagyu that when they had been walking he had thought to himself how easily his master might be attacked while looking at the cherry trees, despite his skill as a master swordsman. Yagyu smiled and said that he understood what had happened and forgave the youth for having disturbed him.

Peril of the ninja

Zanshin was vital if dealing with enemies such as the ninja (practitioners of the 'art of invisibility'), whose talents made them formidable intelligence agents and assassins.

Expert in the use of weapons and skilled in the use of poisons and explosives, a ninja collected information on potential enemies, discovered their weaknesses and set out to exploit them.

Female ninja could use their sexual attractiveness to disarm a victim and then kill him. Eda Hachiro, a young male ninja, exploited the homosexual preferences of the abbot of Kumano in order to steal a rare Chinese manuscript on military methods.

Lavish devices were installed in castles to deter ninja. A special feature of Nijo Castle in Kyoto is the 'nightingale floor' which emits high pitched squeaks when anyone walks on it, thereby alerting the inhabitants to a ninja's presence. The floor was installed to act as an alarm if anyone approached the inner chambers without permission, and thus the guards would be prepared to attack intruders.

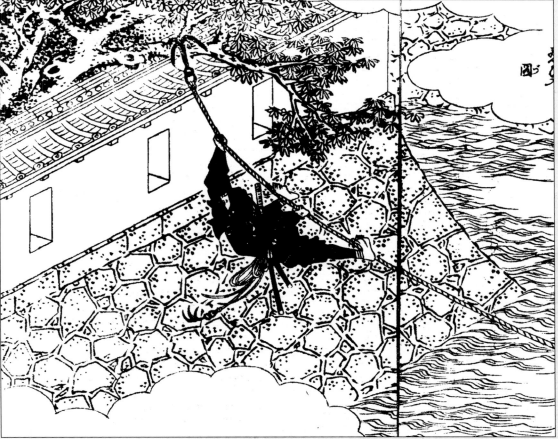

Above: One of the best known of ninja 'magic tricks' involved strange signs made by the fingers, designed to hypnotise an enemy, or to give the ninja a sudden surge of mystic power.

Left: The earliest known illustration of a ninja as a man in black is this section from the 'Ehon Taiko-ki', an illustrated life of Toyotomi Hideyoshi, printed in 1802. The caption reads 'Kimura Hitachi No Suke enters Fushimi Castle in secret'.

The Hogen Incident

On July 29, 1156, the night-time attack advocated by Tametomo was carried out instead by Emperor Go-Shirakawa's forces. During the fighting, known as the Hogen Incident, Tametomo distinguished himself by numerous feats of martial prowess. One of his 'turnip-headed' arrows sliced Oba Kageyoshi's leg off, and continued on its way, finally striking a horse.

Before the battle, Yamada Koreyuki, a samurai from Iga province who was known as 'The Wild Boar' because of his aggressive spirit, dismissed Tametomo with the words: 'Suppose it is Tametomo's arrow, it won't pierce my armour. I at least can let myself be hit'. In the resulting archery duel, Tametomo's arrow pierced the front of Yamada Koreyuki's saddle, went through his armour and his body, and pinned him to the back of the saddle.

The Hogen Incident ended when the Shirakawa-den was set on fire. Sutoku's followers either died in the flames, ran away, or were killed by Minamoto Yoshitomo's archers. Some of the leaders were captured and executed, including Minamoto Tametoshi, who was beheaded on the orders of his son, Yoshitomo. The ex-Emperor Sutoku was sent into exile, where he spent his time making copies of Buddhist sutras. Utterly disheartened by his fate, he went mad and died, aged 46, in 1164. Yoshitomo showed mercy to his younger brother, Tametomo, who was banished after having the tendons of his arm severed to prevent him from ever firing a bow again.

Although Emperor Go-Shirakawa held the throne, it was Taira Kiyomori who emerged from the Hogen Incident as the power behind the throne. Infuriating his Minamoto allies, Kiyomori adopted the Fujiwara policy of providing the imperial line with wives and concubines, and attempted to manipulate the imperial family in the interests of the Taira. Emperor Go-Shirakawa abdicated in favour of his son, who became Emperor Nijo. Once again, Japan had a Cloistered Emperor.

Below: The burning of the Sanjo palace during the 'Heiji Insurrection' of 1160. Samurai search the blazing building to find more victims to decapitate.

TAMETOMO'S LAST STAND

Tametomo died as he had lived, defiantly facing his enemies with his bow and arrow in his hand. During his exile, Tametomo's arm healed and he was able to return to his life as a warrior. In April 1170, Emperor Go-Shirakawa sent a strong force of Taira samurai to bring Tametomo to heel.

As the Taira ships approached, Tametomo dismissed his soldiers, giving each one a keepsake, and went to face his enemies alone. The great archer was regretting how little harm he could do to the approaching forces when a ship, laden with enemy warriors, sailed into view. Taking up his bow, Tametomo fired his last shot at the Taira ship. The arrow went straight through the hull just above the waterline, causing it to sink quickly and drowning many of the 300 Taira warriors on board. The other ships put out to sea for safety. Pleased that his last shot had been so successful, Tametomo entered his house and killed himself by slicing open his abdomen with his dagger, thereby establishing the tradition of seppuku, which would feature prominently in the samurais' code of honour throughout their later history.

Below: The act of seppuku, or hara-kiri, of which the first recorded act in Japanese history was performed by the archer Minamoto Tametomo.

The Heiji Insurrection

The Minamoto clan were bitterly disappointed by the aftermath of the Hogen Incident and direct struggle between the Taira and the Minamoto became inevitable. The scene was set for a sequence of events known as the Heiji Insurrection.

On January 14, 1160, Kiyomori and his son left Kyoto to go on a pilgrimage to Kumano. Five days after he had left, the Minamoto, in league with some Fujiwara allies, seized ex-Emperor Go-Shirakawa and his young son, Emperor Nijo, setting fire to the imperial palace in the process. The first stage of the Minamoto plan had succeeded; with the emperor under their control, they could oppose the Taira without being branded rebels.

But the Minamoto's moment of glory was brief. Kiyomori hurried back to Kyoto, where his forces began to regain control of the capital. The Minamoto cause was lost when both emperors escaped and returned to the protection of the Taira. Minamoto Yoshitomo was taken prisoner and executed, and his eldest son, Yoritomo, was sent to Izu to be adopted by a Taira family. Kiyomori spared the lives of the three younger brothers, but only on the condition that their mother, Tokiwa, became his concubine. The three boys were sent to various monasteries to be trained as priests.

It seemed that nothing could challenge Taira supremacy. The only adult Minamoto warrior still alive after Tametomo died in 1170 was Yorimasa, who had refused to become involved in the insurrection. Yoshitomo's sons were under Taira control, and in 1180, Kiyomori's grandson came to the throne as Emperor Antoku. Taira control seemed complete. But the samurai had a saying to remind them that danger was never far away: 'katte kabuto-no o shimeyo' ('after victory tighten your helmet cords').

DEATH BEFORE DISHONOUR

Right: The Japanese dagger, or tanto, which, along with the similar akuchi (which has no guard) would be the normally preferred weapon for seppuku.

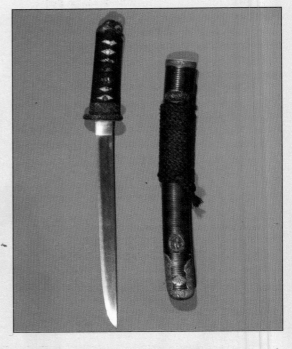

Death for the samurai was not something to be feared. As warriors, they devoted themselves to fighting, and when death came it was expected that they would face it with courage and strength.

Daidoji Yuzan (1639-1730) wrote in 'The Budo Shoshinshu' ('Collection for Beginners in the Way of the Warrior'): 'For the man who would be a warrior, regardless of high or low rank, his very first consideration should be the quality of his physical end, when his fate runs out'.

This willingness to embrace death finds an echo in the Roman custom of a defeated general falling on his sword, or the tradition in the British army of a disgraced officer shooting himself rather than face a court martial. 'Death before dishonour' was a phrase that the samurai would have understood well. Rather than allow himself to be shamed by being taken prisoner and beheaded by his enemies, the tradition arose among the samurai of disembowelling himself with his own sword.

In time, this custom (known as seppuku — a more dignified form of the expression 'hara-kiri', or 'cutting of the belly') became the accepted form of death in a number of different circumstances: to prevent the humiliation of capture by an enemy; as an act of kanshi (a form of remonstration to a superior); or as a death sentence imposed by the authorities.

On occasion, it was also performed as an act of junshi (suicide on the death of a lord). When

Below: The dramatic suicide performed by Imai Kunehira at the Battle of Awazu in 1184, where his master, Minamoto 'Kiso' Yoshinaka, was defeated.

Emperor Meiji died in 1912, General Nogi, one of the heroes of the Russo-Japanese War, committed seppuku as an act of junshi, leaving behind him a poem which read:
'After the great Lord who has passed from the floating world,
I would go following his shadow'.
The first recorded act of seppuku was the death of Minamoto Tametomo, in 1170. Ten years later, another Minamoto samurai, Yorimasa, took his own life at the Byodoin Temple near Kyoto. He wrote a poem of farewell, knelt on his iron fan and pushed his sword into his abdomen.

This excruciatingly painful method of suicide became the approved style in the centuries that followed. It was chosen for a number of reasons. It could only be performed correctly by a man of great courage, thereby distinguishing the performer as a member of the military élite. Also, the stomach (or hara) is thought of by the Japanese as the physical and spiritual centre of the body, and the hara was therefore the natural place to cut to cause death.

In time, a ritual became established, with all aspects of the act clearly defined. To avoid prolonging the performer's pain, he was helped by another man, known as a kaishakunin. The kaishakunin's role was to behead the performer as the act was completed, or if it seemed that the performer's courage might falter at the critical moment. The kaishkunin had to be a skilled swordsman as he was expected to leave the head attached to the body by an uncut section of the neck, so that it could not be mistaken for an ordinary execution.

THE WITNESS

In 1868, the ceremony of seppuku was witnessed by Lord Redesdale, then a young British diplomat in Japan. A Bizen samurai, Taki Zenzaburo, had been ordered to commit seppuku for the crime of firing upon foreign settlements in Hyogo (the modern city of Kobe). In his memoirs, 'Tales of Old Japan', Lord Redesdale gives a detailed account of the ceremony:

'Slowly, and with great dignity, the condemned man mounted on to the raised floor, prostrated himself before the high alter twice, and seated himself before the felt carpet with his back to the high altar, the kaishaku crouching on his left-hand side.

'One of the three attendant officers then came forward, bearing a stand... on which lay the wakisashi, the short sword or dirk of the Japanese. This he handed... to the condemned man, who received it reverently, raising it to his head with both hands, and placed it in front of himself.

'...[the condemned man] allowed his upper garments to slip down to his girdle and remained naked to the waist. Carefully, according to custom, he tucked his sleeves under his knees to prevent himself from falling backwards, for a noble Japanese gentleman should die falling forwards. Deliberately, with a steady hand, he took the dirk that lay before him; he looked at it wistfully, almost affectionately; for a moment he seemed to collect his thoughts for the last time, and then, stabbing himself deeply below the waist on the left-hand side, he drew the dirk slowly across to the right side, and, turning it in the wound, gave a slight cut upwards.

'During this sickeningly painful operation, he never moved a muscle of his face. When he drew out the dirk, he leaned forward and stretched out his neck; an expression of pain for the first time crossed his face, but he uttered no sound.

'At that moment, the kaishaku, who... had been keenly watching his every movement, sprang to his feet, poised his sword for a second in the air; there was a flash, a heavy, ugly thud, a crashing fall; with one blow the head had been severed from the condemned man's body.

'A silence followed, broken only by the hideous noise of the blood throbbing out of the inert heap before us, which but a moment before had been a brave and chivalrous man'.

Below: A samurai prepares to commit seppuku, with his second and his accuser looking on, in this Meiji photograph posed in a studio by models.

The Rise to Power

The Gempei War

The Gempei War of 1180-85 takes its name from the Chinese reading of the characters for Minamoto (Genji) and Taira (Heike). Taira Kiyomori's decision to allow Yoshitomo's sons to live was a mistake. Although one died young, three of the boys grew to manhood, and they all swore to overthrow the Taira and restore the fortunes of their clan.

Minamoto Yoshitsune, a great, if tragic, figure in the history of the samurai, vowed at the age of 11 to revenge his father and restore his clan. It is said that he showed no interest in his education until the abbot of the temple where he had been placed introduced him to the Chinese military classic 'The Art of War', by Sun Tzu, and other similar works. He then became a model pupil in order to prepare himself for the task ahead.

In 1180, at the age of 74, Minamoto Yorimasa rose in revolt against the Taira with the support of Prince Monchihito, the second son of ex-Emperor Go-Shirakawa, who joined forces with the Minamoto in an attempt to take the throne for himself. On May 5, 1180, Prince Monchihito issued a proclamation calling for

help to overthrow the Taira. Describing the Taira as robbers and usurpers who had defied the emperor, despoiled imperial graves and destroyed the Buddhist law, Prince Monchihito called for: 'those of the Minamoto, the Fujiwara and the brave now living in the provinces of the three circuits, now add their efforts to the cause. If there be those who perform meritoriously, dispatch missions to me and inform me of their names and deeds. I shall, without fail, following my enthronement, bestow rewards upon them according to their wishes. Proclaim this message in all the provinces and carry out the terms of this pronouncement'.

The alliance gained the support of the warrior monks of Mii-dera (Mii Temple), but at first they were hopelessly outnumbered by the Taira forces and forced to flee from Kyoto, pursued by large numbers of Taira samurai. Crossing the River Uji, they decided to make a stand using the natural defence of the river to their advantage. They ripped up the planking of the bridge in order to hamper the Taira advance, and, putting the Prince in a nearby temple, the Byodoin, to rest, they waited for the Taira army to reach them.

Below left: According to legend, the future shogun of Japan, Minamoto Yoritomo, was reluctant to take up arms against the Taira clan until this dramatic incident in 1179, when the priest called Mongaku Shonin presented him with the head of his father, Minamoto Yoshitomo.

Below right: An ivory statuette depicting two lower-class warriors grappling using characteristic arms and armour of the period.

JOMYO MEISHU

Fought in an age that was riddled with tales of superhuman bravery, the Battle of Uji gave rise to its own share of such legends.

The 'Heike Monogatari' ('Tale of the Heike'), a collection of military histories written between 1221 and 1371, relates how one warrior monk, Jomyo Meishu, displaying tremendous contempt for his opponents, walked out onto the timbers of the bridge and, with his favourite white-handled halberd in his hands, challenged the Taira to fight him.

'In a mighty voice he named his name, saying: "You have long heard of me, now take a good look. I am Tsutsui no Jomyo Meishu, known to all of Mii temple as a warrior worth a thousand men. Let those who will advance, and we shall see the outcome", and he then mercilessly let fly his 24 arrows.

'Immediately, 12 warriors fell dead and 11 were wounded, and still one arrow remained in his quiver. He threw down his bow and stripped off his quiver. Then, kicking off his foot-gear, he sprang barefoot onto the beams of the bridge, and charged across.

None would advance to meet him, and Jomyo proceeded, as though strolling the wide streets of the capital'.

During the fighting, it is said that Jomyo killed around 26 Taira warriors with his bow, naginata, sword and knife; when he retired from the fighting, he had 63 enemy arrows sticking out of his armour, none of which, apparently, had caused him any serious harm.

Below: A painted screen depicting Sasaki Takatsuna (on left) racing Kajiwara Kagesue for the honour of being first into battle by crossing the River Uji. Note the Uji bridge in the background, from which the planking has been removed as a defence.

The Battle of Uji

As dawn broke on June 20, 1180, the Taira forces arrived at the River Uji, but due to the thick early morning mist the opposing armies could only locate each other by the sound of their war cries.

The Taira sent some horsemen to capture the bridge, but they were blinded by the mist and charged straight through the broken planking and into the river. Then, as the mist cleared, a great archery duel took place over the river, the warrior monks proving to be formidable archers.

Unable to force their way across the bridge, the Taira began to consider making a 80.5 km (50 miles) detour to the bridge at Setsa, but one of the Taira allies, Ashikaga no Taira Tadatsuna, eventually managed to ford the river with 300 of his followers and established a bridgehead that allowed the bulk of the Taira army to cross.

The Minamoto forces began to fall back and, anticipating defeat, Minamoto Yorimasa and his son, Nakatsuna, committed seppuku. Prince Monchihito escaped but was later killed by Taira archers. The Battle of Uji resulted in a Taira victory.

Taira Kiyomori proceeded to take his revenge on all the rebels, publicly displaying the heads of Prince Monchihito and Yorimasa's sons in Kyoto and, in December 1180, he sent a force of 10,000 Taira samurai to punish the monks of Mii-dera for having supported the Minamoto rebellion.

The Youngest Son

Perhaps the greatest individual to feature in the Gempei War was the youngest of Yoshitomo's sons, Minamoto Yoshitsune. Certainly, he has captured the imagination of Japanese writers for the past eight centuries, who have seen in him the model of the perfect samurai.

Yoshitsune was born in 1159 and after the death of his father, he was sent to the monastery of Kurama-dera to be educated as a Buddhist priest. But the young boy much preferred the martial arts to learning Buddhist sutras. According to legend, he would slip out of the temple at night to receive lessons in sword fighting from the 'tengu' in secret

Below: The young Yoshitsune is taught sword-fighting by the tengu of the forests of Mount Kurama.

places in the forest. (The tengu are mythical creatures, which have the beak, wings and eyes of a hawk and the body, arms and legs of a man. By tradition, they are the guardians of the mysteries of the martial arts.)

At the age of 15, Yoshitsune left the temple to perform his manhood ceremony. He went to the home of his sponsor, Fujiwara Hidehira, whose lands lay north of Honshu. On the way he had many adventures, fighting and killing bandits and, at one point, seducing the daughter of a Taira lord in order to gain access to a rare Chinese work on warfare.

One night in Kyoto, he was crossing the Gojo bridge when he was stopped by a warrior monk. The monk, whose name was Benkei, had resolved to collect 1000 sword blades; Yoshitsune's weapon would have completed his collection, and he demanded that the youth hand over his sword. Yoshitsune refused and so they began to fight. Using his tengu-taught skills, Yoshitsune avoided Benkei's attacks and brought him to his knees, but instead of killing him, Yoshitsune spared his life. Benkei bowed deeply to his new master, and swore to serve Yoshitsune to the death.

The relationship between the great samurai Yoshitsune and his faithful follower Benkei has become a central theme of Japanese art and literature, encapsulating the values of courage and loyalty that were so important to the culture of the samurai class.

Brothers in arms

When the struggle against the Taira began in 1180, Yoshitsune offered his services to his brother Yoritomo. Instead of directing him against the Taira, Yoritomo set him against their cousin, Yoshinaka, whom Yoritomo, characteristically, feared as a possible rival to his position as head of the Minamoto clan. In 1184, after Yoshinaka had put Go-Shirakawa back on the throne, forces commanded by Yoshitsune and his elder brother, Noriyori, engaged Yoshinaka's army in battle at the River Uji.

Yoshinaka's forces were defeated in the battle and he committed seppuku, leaving Yoritomo free to devote his full attention to destroying the Taira. He entrusted this task to Yoshitsune who, by a brilliant series of offensive techniques, which featured rapid surprise attacks by small numbers of warriors, defeated the Taira at the Battle of Ichi-no-tani, in February 1184. A year later, Yoshitsune took the fight deep into Taira territory, attacking the Taira headquarters at Yashima on the northern coast of Shikoku.

With 150 carefully chosen warriors he approached the Taira stronghold under the cover of a storm. Attacking as the sun rose, Yoshitsune's samurai set buildings on fire and cut down anyone who opposed them.

The Taira panicked and fled to their ships, taking the boy-emperor, Antoku, with them. During the Battle of Yashima, one Taira samurai

UNITED IN COMBAT

During the fighting at the River Uji, Minamoto Yoshinaka was supported by his wife, Tomoe Gozen, a redoubtable warrior in her own right, and by his brother-in-law, Imai Kunehira. When it was obvious that all was lost, Yoshinaka and his few remaining retainers charged in desperation against Yoshitsune's samurai.

Tomoe Gozen insisted on remaining on the battlefield to face defeat alongside Yoshinaka, telling him: 'I want to fight the last glorious fight in front of you'. The 'Heike Monogatari' records that, facing a powerful enemy warrior, she 'flung herself upon Onda and, grappling with him, dragged him from his horse... and cut off his head'.

She then told her husband that she would hold off the enemy while he withdrew to commit seppuku so he could not be taken prisoner. But as he went, Yoshinaka's horse became stuck in deep mud and he was hit by an arrow in the face, his head being removed by two of Yoshitsune's followers. Upon seeing this, Imai Kunehira killed himself by putting the point of his sword in his mouth and jumping off his horse so that the blade pierced his brain.

Tomoe's fate after the battle is uncertain, but it is generally thought that she retired to a convent, where she devoted the rest of her life to reading Buddhist sutras and praying for the good of Yoshinaka's spirit.

Left: Tomoe Gozen, wife of Minamoto Yoshinaka and the most famous samurai woman in Japanese history.

fastened a fan painted with a red sun disc to the mast of his ship and challenged the Minamoto to fire at it. An 18-year-old samurai, Nasu Munetaka, stepped forward, took aim and fired. His well-aimed arrow shattered the fan and from that point on, Munetaka's descendants adopted the design of a fan bearing a sun disc as their mon, or family crest

Left: The Battle of Yashima, in 1184, at which Minamoto Yoshitsune gained the second victory of his campaign against the Taira.

FEMALE SAMURAI

Far right: A woman armed only with a naginata puts to flight the samurai who have attacked her home.

Below: Two women fighting with wooden staves, practice weapons known as jo.

In general, samurai society was dominated by men, but history records that the female members of the samurai clans often displayed a fighting spirit and a concern for honour and duty matching that of the men. Women were trained in the martial arts and, in time, many became highly skilled, especially in the use of the naginata.

Tales of courageous and devoted samurai women abound in the epic 'Heike Monogatari'. Chief among these is Minamoto Yoshinaka's wife, Tomoe Gozen, but the period produced numerous other heroic samurai women, including Hojo Masako, the wife of Minamoto Yoritomo, who was known as 'the general in nun's habit' (on her husband's death, she became a Buddhist nun, the traditional fate of samurai widows). Masako was a prominent political player in the early years of the Hojo regency that succeeded her husband, at one point engaging in open conflict with her father. From her new position as a Buddhist nun, she successfully bullied the samurai chiefs into standing by the shogunate.

These histories reflect the relatively strong position women held in samurai society at the time. Laws governing the shogun's court in the early 13th century allowed women equal rights of inheritance with brothers and the right to bequeath property. Samurai and bushi wives had high status in the household. They controlled household expenditure, managed servants, and were called upon to defend the home in times of war. They were also responsible for raising their children to the samurai ideals of contempt for death and unquestioning loyalty to their lord.

'A creature of... no importance'

Over the centuries that followed, the practice of using daughters as pawns in the marriage market (a crucial tool in the struggles of the period) and the influence of neo-Confucian philosophy, combined to reduce the status of female samurai. The ideal of fearless devotion was gradually replaced by one of quiet passive obedience, a change reflected by the introduction of new words for wife: kanai and okusan (persons in the innermost recesses of the house).

By the 17th century, many samurai felt that, while women were necessary to bear children, they were not really fitting companions for warriors. A cult of homosexuality developed among some warriors and, despite repeated prohibition, many adult samurai formed close relationships with men. In 1687, Ihara Saikaku published his famous book 'Nanshoku Okagami' ('The Great Mirror of Manly Love'), which took homosexual activity among the samurai as its theme. 'Woman is a creature of absolutely no importance', he wrote, 'but sincere pederastic love is true love'.

Samurai women were still expected to show contempt for death when it came to defending their husbands' honour. A wife's sacrifice of herself, or her honour, for the sake of her husband was a common theme in Japanese drama. Self-renunciation was an imperative for women and remained so even at the end of the 19th century, despite the popularity of Western ideas.

Inanzo Nitobe, writing in 1905, devoted one chapter of his book 'Bushido: The Soul of Japan' to 'The Training and Position of Women'. This

あの阿能の局英戦殿頻

underlines the inferior role accorded to women, telling us that: 'In the ascending scale of service stood woman, who annihilated herself for a man, that he might annihilate himself for the master, that he in turn might obey Heaven'.

However, the fighting spirit of female samurai still managed to show itself on occasion. Their martial prowess was demonstrated during the Satsuma Rebellion of 1877, when the women of Kagoshima fought against the imperial army. In 1868, the fighting between supporters of the shogunate and those supporting the imperial restoration provided another such display.

Samurai of the Aizu clan, supporters of the shogunate, were left to defend their stronghold of Wakamatsu Castle without any hope of outside assistance. Heavily outnumbered by an army of 20,000 men, the 3000 Aizu samurai mobilised anyone who could use a weapon. A group of 20 women formed a unit that fought on the front line.

One of the women, Nakano Takeko, was highly skilled in the use of the naginata, and during the fighting she rushed into the enemy lines and cut down many men. Eventually she was shot in the chest. To avoid the disgrace of capture, she told her sister Yuko to remove her head and take it home.

A monument to her was erected in the Hokai temple in Aizu Bangemachi, Fukishima province.

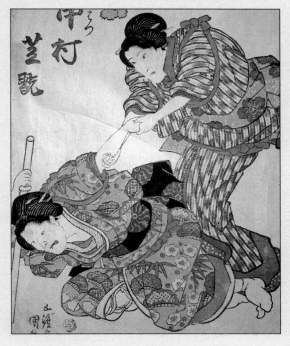

Left: In this theatrical print by Kunisada, two women (roles played by men on the stage) are depicted in unarmed combat. One applies a ju-jutsu armlock to the other.

Right: The suicide of Taira Tomomori after losing the Battle of Dan-no-Ura. Note the heike crabs in the foreground.

The Victorious Minamoto

After their defeat at Yashima, the bedraggled Taira forces made their way to their last major stronghold at Hikoshima. Yoshitsune's success meant that he attracted the support and allegiance of many samurai leaders anxious to be on the side of the victorious Minamoto. Among his allies, Yoshitsune could count on the support of a number of skilled sailors whose ships were needed to carry the Minamoto forces to the final decisive battle with the Taira.

Yoshitsune spent some time reorganising and training his troops and on the morning of April 25, 1184, the Taira and Minamoto fleets clashed off the coast of Honshu, opposite a beach known as Dan-no-ura. The Taira fleet, commanded by Taira Tomomori, numbered about 400 ships, while the Minamoto and their allies had about 850. Neither the Taira nor the Minamoto fleets displayed any real naval tactics; the ships were simply floating platforms from which archers could engage in exchanges of arrows until the ships came close and man-to-man combat could take place.

At first, the Taira seemed to gain the advantage, but the tide changed and began to push their ships towards the beach. At that point, one of the Taira samurai, Taguchi Shigeyoshi, abandoned the Taira cause, pulling down the red flag of the Taira and raising the white flag of the Minamoto. His last-minute defection enabled Yoshitsune to

Below: Taira Noritsune pursues Minamoto Yoshitsune from boat to boat during the Battle of Dan-no-Ura.

discover quickly which of the Taira ships held Emperor Antoku, and soon all of the Minamoto ships concentrated on capturing that single vessel.

The death of the emperor

Realising that everything was lost, Taira Tomomori went to the boy-emperor and told him that death

was the only solution. The emperor's grandmother picked up the eight-year-old boy in her arms, walked to the side of the ship, and after saying a prayer to their ancestors and Buddha, stepped off the ship and disappeared into the waves.

The young emperor's death was the signal for the Taira to commit mass-suicide. The emperor's mother attempted to follow her son but was dragged out of the sea by a Minamoto samurai, who used a rake to ensnare her hair. Five of the leading members of the Taira family attached heavy anchors to their armour and jumped into the sea, but the head of the clan, Munenori, refused to follow their example.

One of the Taira samurai, angered by his leader's lack of courage, pushed him into the sea, but Munenori managed to swim until he was captured by a Minamoto vessel. Before she drowned, Munenori's mother (the emperor's grandmother) is said to have explained his lack of courage by revealing that he was not a true Taira but the son of an umbrella merchant, exchanged at birth for a baby girl.

The Taira fleet commander, Tomomori, was the last of the Taira leaders to die; he put on two suits of armour to weigh himself down and followed his family into the waves. Taira Munenori's cowardice did not help him; Yoshitsune executed him, his son, and the last surviving son of Kiyomori, within a few weeks of the Taira defeat.

The Taira were devastated by the Battle of Dan-no-ura and they never again rose to any positions of power. Many of the surviving members of the clan later became vassals of Minamoto Yoritomo. According to legend, the ghosts of the Taira haunted the area of Dan-no-ura and the heike-gani, large crabs found in the sea around the area, were said to contain the souls of the drowned samurai.

Minamoto Yoritomo was now the virtual ruler of Japan. Instead of settling in Kyoto near the emperor, Yoritomo established his own centre of government in Kamakura.

The emperor remained in Kyoto, but real power was to be found with Yoritomo in Kamakura. Known as the Bakufu (camp office), it was, in the words of the British historian Stephen Turnbull, 'a government of the samurai, by the samurai and for the samurai'.

Above: Taira Noritsune prepares to jump into the sea and commit suicide while fighting off three Minamoto samurai.

The Bakufu

Left: Emperor
Go-Toba, whose long
reign witnessed some
of the most dramatic
developments in
samurai history.

To prevent his warriors from being corrupted by life at the Kyoto court, Yoritomo established an alternative government of his own in Kamakura. He accorded the emperor all the respect and loyalty due to his position, as long as the emperor was content to be a figurehead, but there was no doubt in anyone's mind where the real power lay.

In 1192, the ex-Emperor Go-Shirakawa died and his thirteen-year-old grandson, Go-Toba, was left, theoretically, to rule the country. Ever-eager to bolster his authority, Yoritomo made his wishes known to the young emperor and, three months

Left: Emperor Go-Toba, whose long reign witnessed some of the most dramatic developments in samurai history.

Below: A portrait of Minamoto Yoritomo in full court costume.

after the death of Go-Shirakawa, he was bestowed with the rank of shogun. Normally this rank was awarded on a temporary basis, but Yoritomo turned it into an hereditary office; his role as military dictator was legitimised and he set about strengthening his position.

For ambitious men with administrative and legal skills, the new government in Kamakura presented splendid opportunities for advancement. The fighting skills of the samurai may have won the battles, but the literary skills of scholars were needed to administer the peace. Scholars soon found employment with the Bakufu, among them Oe Hiromoto, a member of a family that had served the imperial house for hundreds of years.

The skills of these men were put to good use and an administrative system was set up, based on three main organs of government. The samurai-dokoro was a court of honour for the samurai. It decided on promotions, correct behaviour, battle tactics and planning, and the ethics expected of a true samurai. The man-dokoro was responsible for general administration and the day-to-day running of the Bakufu; in effect, it was Yoritomo's civil service, and its first president was Oe Hiromoto.

The monchu-jo was a judicial body, intended to serve as the final court of appeal in land disputes that could not be dealt with locally by the

THE HOJO REGENTS

Yoritomo was succeeded by his two sons, Yoriie and Sanetomo. Their mother, Masako, set up a council of regents headed by her father, Hojo Tokimasa, which was intended to advise and assist with the tasks of government. Neither of the sons proved capable of the task and real power fell into the hands of the Hojo family. They became the power behind the shogunate, taking the title of shikken (or regent), although they never took the title of shogun.

Yoritomo's legacy had dwindled into a bewildering collection of dummy rulers, neatly summarised by George Sansom as 'a state at the head of which stands a titular emperor whose vestigial functions are usurped by an abdicated emperor, and whose real power is nominally delegated to an hereditary military dictator but actually wielded by an hereditary adviser of that dictator'.

The Hojo regents followed Yoritomo's policy of providing strong government. The assassination of the third shogun, Minamoto Sanetomo, in 1219, led to the selection of a two-year-old boy, Fujiwara Yoritsune, as the next holder of the office. This in turn led Emperor Go-Toba to believe that he could overthrow the Bakufu and restore imperial power. He began to assemble troops from the nobility, Buddhist temples, Shinto shrines and his own palace guards, and he hoped to win the loyalty of many of the vassals of the Bakufu.

While Go-Toba was reasonably successful in winning the support of the samurai in the Kyoto area, the powerful clans of the Kanto rejected his overtures and when, in 1221, he began the Shokyu War, he was attacked by three armies, which converged on Kyoto and destroyed his forces. The war lasted less than a month and resulted in Go-Toba's exile to the islands of Oki, where he spent his time writing poetry until his death in 1239.

The Bakufu emerged as the only real government of Japan, dictating not only who would be shogun, but also who would occupy the throne.

Below: This finely-observed wooden sculpture portrays Hojo Tokiyori, shikken (regent for the shogun) between 1246 and 1256. He is depicted wearing the black headgear of the 13th-century court.

constables or stewards appointed by the shogun. Evidently, Yoritomo had learned some lessons from history and did not want squabbles over land to escalate into warfare, as had so often happened in the past. In general, his system worked and claims were dealt with fairly.

Other aspects of his rule were less commendable. Yoritomo's anxiety about the intentions of his relatives led him to execute another of his half-brothers, Noriyori, in 1193. His policy of slaughtering his immediate family as their usefulness diminished steadily eroded the leadership of his clan, and when, in 1199, he was thrown from his horse and died of his injuries, there was a severe shortage of talented male Minamoto to take his place.

Legend has it that Yoritomo's death was caused by Yoshitsune's ghost, whose appearance caused the horse to rear, thereby providing Yoshitsune with his revenge on the man who had treated him so cruelly.

Left: The grave of Minamoto Yoritomo in his capital of Kamakura.

The Mongol Invasions

The Mongols

Below: Mongol armies lay siege to a citadel in this exquisite Persian miniature of the period.

Before the 12th century, the Mongol people were divided into small tribes of pastoral nomads living to the north of the Great Wall of China. Their lives revolved around acquiring enough pasture and water to keep their flocks alive, and when necessary they fought small inter-tribal wars to take what they needed.

In 1162, a child was born who was destined to forge the scattered tribes into a mighty war machine that would conquer an empire reaching from the Arctic to the Red Sea, and from the Volga River to China. His name was Temuchin, but by the time he died, in 1227, he was better known as Genghis Khan.

The Mongol army was essentially composed of armoured archers mounted on small, tough ponies. Mongol warriors were drilled to fight in highly disciplined groups, executing precise manoeuvres to commands relayed by drums, gongs and bells.

The Venetian traveller Marco Polo described their battle tactics: '...never do they mix directly with their enemies, but keep hovering about their sides, discharging their arrows from one side and then from the other. And on occasion they pretend to flee; during their flight, they shoot backward at their pursuers, thereby killing many men and horses'.

No army in the world could stand up to the speed, shock and ferocity exhibited by the Mongols and for a time the momentum of their conquests seemed unstoppable. By 1259, the Mongols had conquered Korea and, in 1271, Kublai Khan, the grandson of Genghis Khan, established Mongol rule in China by founding the Yuan dynasty. In 1268, Kublai Khan sent emissaries to the Japanese with demands that they acknowledge the Mongols as their overlords by sending tribute to the Mongol court.

Most countries welcomed such tributary relations with China as their economies benefited from the resulting trade. However, the Japanese refused to accept the inferior position that sending tribute indicated, and the Hojo regent, Masamura, sent the Mongol envoys back to China with a rejection of the Great Khan's demands. Predictably, Kublai Khan was very angry; he was not used to having his demands refused and so he decided to punish the Japanese for their defiance.

'A real lion roar'

The Mongols began to assemble an army composed of Mongol, Chinese and Korean soldiers and, in November 1274, they set sail from Korea for the island of Tsushima. By this time,

THE CHINESE CONNECTION

Much of Japanese culture and civilisation finds its roots in the culture of China. The unification of the Chinese states, effected by Chin Shih Huang-ti in 221 BC, was followed by remarkable political and cultural developments under the Han emperors (206 BC-AD 220), which reached new heights of sophistication under the T'ang dynasty (AD 618-907).

To the newly emerging Japanese state, the achievements already accomplished by the Chinese were dazzling, and it was to China that the rulers of Japan turned for guidance on systems of government, writing, religion, medicine, metallurgy and many other aspects of their civilisation.

Japan's adoption of Chinese models confirmed the Chinese in their belief that China — the 'Middle Kingdom' — was destined to rule the world because of the superior virtue of her institutions. To the Chinese, it was obvious that only the emperor in Peking embodied the Mandate of Heaven and was therefore not only ruler of China but also of the whole world.

The Japanese rejected this idea completely; while they were willing to learn from the superior culture of China, they would never accept the idea that the ruler of China was their overlord and someone to whom they should pay homage. After all, the rulers of Japan were descended from the gods and were divine beings themselves.

Left: The Emperor Chin Shih Huang-ti, who unified the Chinese states.

Hojo Masamura had retired from the post of regent to become chief of staff of the Bakufu, and been replaced by Hojo Tokimune, an 18-year-old samurai of great ability.

Tokimune was a follower of the Zen master Bukko (1226-86), a Chinese teacher of Buddhism who had already faced up to the Mongols in China. A detachment of Mongol soldiers had entered a temple where Bukko was sitting in meditation, and drawn their swords to cut him down. Without displaying any fear, Bukko recited a poem which he composed at that moment:

'In heaven and earth, no crack to hide;
Joy to know that man is void and things
    too are void.
Splendid the great Mongolian longsword,
It's lightning flash cuts the spring
    breeze'.

Legend has it that the Mongol warriors were so impressed with his courage that they left him unharmed. Hojo Tokimune left a record of his studies under Bukko, known as 'The Grass of the Way', in which he records that when the news came of the Mongol fleet, he went to see Bukko and said, 'The great thing has come'. Bukko asked him, 'Can you somehow avoid it?'. Tokimune stamped his foot and gave a great roar. Bukko said, 'A real lion cub, a real lion roar. Dash straight forward and don't look round!'

Left: Kublai Khan, the leader of the Mongols who ordered the unsuccessful attempts at an invasion of Japan.

The Common Enemy

Hojo Tokimune realised that to resist the Mongol threat the various clans would have to cease their feuding and join together to fight the common enemy. Tokimune was assisted in this respect by recent religious developments. Psychologically, the Japanese had been prepared for the Mongol invasion to some extent by the activities of the Buddhist priest Nichiren (1222-82).

Nichiren wanted to purify Buddhism by stressing the actual words of the Buddha, which he felt could be found in the Lotus Sutra. He sought to create a national Buddhist church, so as he preached he warned the Japanese that unless they abandoned the degenerate practices of the other sects they would be punished by foreign invasion.

The Mongols landed on the islands of Tsushima and Ikishima where, although they met spirited resistance, they simply brushed aside the samurai defenders due to the weight of their numbers. (Tsushima was defended only by a small force of 200 samurai commanded by So Sukekuni, the grandson of Taira Tomomori.)

The Japanese were horrified by the savagery of the Mongols, which was directed indiscriminately at men, women and children. To the samurai, war was the business of warriors and innocent non-combatants should have no part in it; but to the Mongols, terror was one of their most effective weapons, and if butchering civilians gave them victory then, in their eyes, it was quite acceptable.

On November 19, 1274, the Mongol fleet arrived at Hakata Bay and began to land troops at Imazu. They were met by samurai from Kyushu, who began hostilities in their own traditional manner. First an arrow with a humming head was fired to indicate the start of the battle, and then, one by one, the samurai advanced, loudly proclaiming their lineage and courage in order to seek out individual Mongol warriors in man-to-man combat.

The samurai assumed that the Mongols would fight as they did, so that the victors could take heads in order to prove their worth. But the Mongols ignored the formal challenges and arranged themselves into their usual fighting formation, which resembled the ancient Macedonian phalanx.

The Mongols' carefully orchestrated manoeuvres caused many problems for the samurai, who followed their traditional method of charging straight into the enemy. The Mongols dealt with the samurai by firing volleys of poisoned arrows from their short but powerful bows. They also made effective use of spearmen and employed firebombs (probably developed by Chinese military engineers), which were flung from catapults, causing many samurai and their mounts to be badly burned.

Defence walls

The samurai's raw courage was no answer to Mongol tactics and technology, and the defenders were forced to fall back to a defence line of walls, built 600 years before, while they waited for reinforcements to arrive from Shikoku and Honshu.

But the Mongols did not follow up their advantage. They were suffering from a shortage of arrows and the resistance put up by the Japanese was stronger than they had expected. They withdrew to their ships, burning the Hakozaki shrine as they left and destroying a number of villages. As the Mongol fleet left the shelter of Hakata Bay, it was struck by a tremendous storm and was destroyed. It is estimated that the Mongols lost 13,000 men. Their first attempt to

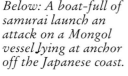

Below: A boat-full of samurai launch an attack on a Mongol vessel lying at anchor off the Japanese coast.

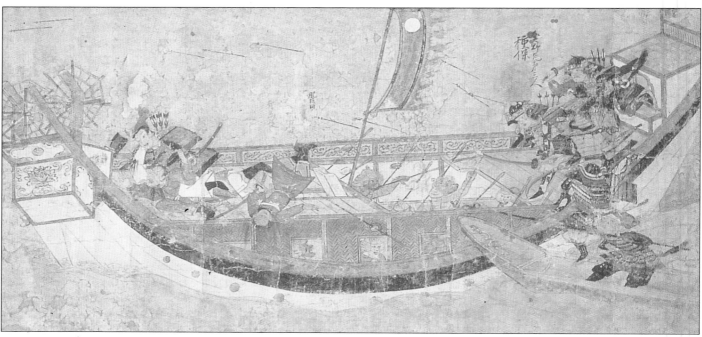

conquer Japan had failed. Any intentions that the Mongols may have had to attempt a second invasion of Japan were temporarily abandoned while they completed the conquest of south China.

By 1279, the Mongol's had established their authority in south China and, once again, Kublai Khan dispatched a mission to demand Japan's submission to him as a vassal state. The Bakufu resolutely opposed his demands, had his envoys' heads removed and began to prepare for the next Mongol onslaught.

The Mongols assembled a huge force of over 140,000 Mongol, Chinese and Korean troops, plus a vast fleet of transports and sailors sent from ports in China and Korea. Meanwhile, mindful of the previous encounter, the Japanese spared no effort in preparing for the attack. They constructed a wall, 4.5 m (15 ft) high and about 40 km (25 miles) in length, along the coast of Hakata Bay and assembled large numbers of small boats and ships to fight the Mongols in the shallow coastal waters. The great Kyushu overlords were ordered to prepare lists of warriors and their equipment so that the Bakufu could have an accurate idea of the numbers and quality of the samurai they could rely on to resist the invaders.

Above: During the lull between the two Mongol invasions, the Japanese built a defensive wall around Hakata Bay from which counter-attacks could be launched.

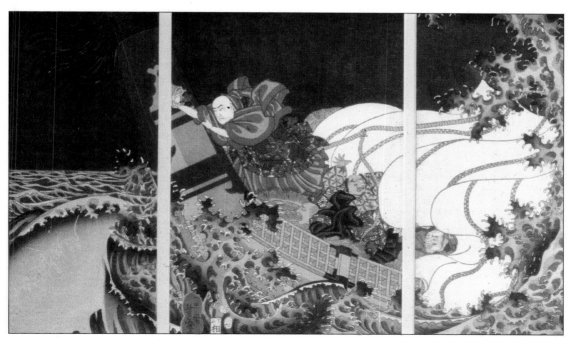

Left: The monk Nichiren, who prophesied the Mongol invasions, pictured here calming a storm by an invocation.

Right: A suit of oyoroi armour, as would have been worn by the samurai who tackled the Mongol invaders.

The Mongols Invade

The Mongols sailed in two groups; a spearhead of 900 ships, carrying over 40,000 men, was followed by the main force of 100,000 men, plus 60,000 sailors, aboard 3500 ships. The first group sailed on May 22, 1281, and arrived at Tsushima on June 9. Again the Japanese resisted strongly but were overcome.

Instead of waiting for the main force to arrive, the Mongol commander decided to attack and headed for Hakata Bay. The Japanese were waiting for them and the samurai resistance was so fierce that even after several days of fighting the Mongols were only able to land in small numbers. True to their aggressive spirit, the samurai were not content to fight a defensive war, and at night they used small boats to raid the Mongol's ships, boarding them and fighting close-in. In one incident, samurai swam out to a ship, climbed on board, and removed the heads of the crew before returning to the shore.

Realising that any attempt to force a landing would prove costly in men and materials, the Mongols withdrew to regroup and attempt a landing elsewhere. The Japanese continued to harass them and then disease spread among the Mongol forces, further weakening them. However, with the larger part of Kublai Khan's fleet due to arrive at any moment, the prospects for a Japanese victory looked bleak. Only a miracle saved Japan.

Below: A battle between Japanese samurai and the Mongol invaders as depicted by Alphonse de Neuville in his 'Le Tour du Monde' of 1866.

A powerful wind wrecked the Mongol ships, entering the history books as one of the most celebrated accidents of history and a cornerstone of Japanese national pride.

Supremacy of the sword

The samurai learned a great deal from fighting the Mongols. The invasions introduced formation combat to the Japanese and the practice began to spread across Japan after this time. The Mongols also influenced the samurai's choice of weapons. The stress on archery lessened and the sword began to assume a more important place in the samurai's fighting skills. Other weapons, such as the spear and naginata, were studied seriously and included in the samurai's arsenal.

Over the next two centuries, the samurai changed from being a mounted archer who used his sword as an auxiliary weapon, to a swordsman who generally fought on foot but could use his archery skills when necessary.

Unrewarded

In normal circumstances, after a successful war the Bakufu could reward its warriors from the lands of its defeated enemies. After the fighting with the Mongols, claims began to flood in from warriors who believed they deserved something for fighting, and from various temples and shrines who were convinced that their prayers had invoked the storm that saved Japan.

KAMI-KAZI

On August 12, 1281, the second wave of Kublai Khan's armada arrived and the Mongol forces combined for the final attack. The Japanese realised that the courage of the samurai would not be enough to prevent such a huge army landing and, in desperation, ex-Emperor Kameyama sent a special envoy to the shrine at Ise to ask his divine ancestress, the Sun Goddess Amaterasu, for her assistance.

It seems that the petition found favour in Amaterasu's eyes for, on August 15, 1281, a powerful wind blew up, which lasted for two days and wreaked terrible destruction upon the Mongol fleet. When this 'kami-kaze' ('divine wind') had blown itself out, the samurai attacked the survivors and successfully defeated the Mongol invasion.

Although the Mongols had lost vast numbers of men and ships, the threat of further invasions remained. The Bakufu was forced to maintain troops and coastal defence works until the death of Kublai Khan in 1300, when the Mongols seem to have abandoned their attempts at an invasion.

The experience of the divine wind did much to strengthen the Japanese in their belief that they enjoyed divine protection. This belief was to endure throughout Japan's later history, even into modern times. It was invoked as a rallying cry for anti-Western samurai in the 19th century; and during World War II, it inspired the conception of the notorious kami-kaze suicide raids.

Below: Amaterasu, the Sun Goddess, reappears from her cave. It was to Amaterasu that the Japanese people prayed to deliver them from the Mongols.

One Kyushu samurai who fought in both invasions had a scroll painted, the 'Moko Shurai Ekotoba' (Mongol Invasion Scroll), depicting his part in the fighting and the journey he took to claim his reward from the Bakufu. After responding so magnificently to the Mongol threat, the samurai found that, in general, the rewards were not generous.

In 1296, 15 years after the first invasion, Kuro Fujiwara Sukekado sent a petition to the Bakufu, in which he complained that: 'During the Mongol attack, I boarded an enemy vessel [at Chigasaki] and, though wounded, took one prisoner. Later, in the attack on Takashima, I took two prisoners. These facts were duly reported to the court of inquiry and witnesses were examined. Yet, though a reward was recommended, I have been left out of the general recognition of merit.... Why should I, who was wounded, have to wait empty for months and years and get nothing for my service?'.

In addition to the sense of disaffection felt by the samurai, the Mongol attacks left agriculture in a weakened state. Consequently, food production fell at precisely the time that the Bakufu needed resources to pay vassals for their service or to reimburse their costs.

For the Bakufu, the aftermath of the invasions presented new dangers. The distress caused by the Mongols had provided supporters of the emperor in Kyoto and disaffected samurai with a common cause: the removal of the Hojo clan from power.

THE WARRIOR MONKS

Far right: These tombs of unknown samurai warriors killed in battle line the approach to the Sugimoto Temple in Kamakura.

Below: 'Tajima the Arrow Cutter', one of the monk-heroes of the Battle of Uji in 1180. Tajima whirled his naginata and cut through the arrows fired at him.

When Emperor Kammu established the new capital of Kyoto in 794, new sects of Buddhism established themselves in the capital and the surrounding countryside. To the northeast of Kyoto stands Mount Hiei, and it was here that a monk named Saicho (767-822), also known by his honorific name of Dengyo Daishi, established the monastery of Enryaku-ji.

In 804, Emperor Kammu sent Saicho to China to study various aspects of Buddhism, in order to find the form of Buddhism most appropriate for the new capital. On his return to Japan, Saicho taught a form of Buddhism that included elements of many different sects, but emphasised the doctrines of the Tendai sect (in Chinese: T'ien-t'ai).

The form of Tendai taught at the Enryaku-ji by Saicho and his followers included the performance of mystical rites, designed to bring wealth, health, longevity and good fortune to the participants. Predictably, it soon attracted a large following. The monastery was accorded

tremendous respect because it was thought to protect the capital from evil influences coming from the unlucky direction of the northeast, known traditionally as the Demon Entrance.

In 891, a power struggle between the followers of two teachers resulted in the establishment of two rival centres of Tendai — one based at Enryaku-ji, known as the Sammon (Mountain Order), and the other at Miidera (also called Onjoji), known as the Jimon (Church Order). As well as internal struggles within the Tendai sect, the monks of Enryaku-ji and Miidera found themselves in dispute with the Buddhist sects based in Nara and with followers of the Shingon (True Word) sect, established by Kukai (774-835) in 816.

As the sects acquired land and wealth through donations from rich and powerful followers, these doctrinal disputes became enmeshed with the more materialistic need to protect their wealth and land from avaricious samurai and government tax collectors.

By the end of the 9th century, the rival branches of the Tendai sect began to recruit akuso (bad monks) to guard their land and temples. Other Buddhist sects followed their example, as did various Shinto shrines, and it soon became normal for all large religious institutions to maintain large standing armies of warrior monks, normally known as sohei.

Scourge of the emperors

The military skills and power of the sohei were so great that even emperors could not ignore the implications of annoying them. Emperor Shirakawa (1053-1129) once said that, although he was the ruler of Japan, there were three things that he could not control; the fall of dice when gambling, the floodwaters of the Kamo River, and the monks of Mount Hiei.

This fear was partly rooted in belief in the monks' magical powers. Emperor Shirakawa, desperate for a son and heir, enlisted the help of Raigo, a Miidera priest who was famous for his magical powers. When Raigo's prayers succeeded, the delighted emperor asked Raigo how he could reward him. Raigo demanded a high price: the right to ordain Tendai priests independently of Enryaku-ji. Concerned not to aggravate the monks of Mount Hiei, Shirakawa refused Raigo's request. His newborn son died shortly afterwards, purportedly as a result of one of Raigo's malevolent spells.

This magical aspect, combined with tremendous martial skills, made the sohei a formidable force. They went into battle wearing monks robes over suits of armour and, while they were skilled archers, they were most famous for their ability with the naginata, a pole arm fitted

with a long sharp blade, sometimes over 1.2 m (4 ft) long. Wielding the weapon in long slashing cuts, they could easily decapitate an enemy, or remove his limbs, with one blow.

One of their tactics when dealing with government opposition was to carry a portable mikoshi (shrine), widely believed to contain the spirit of a god, into the streets of Kyoto and leave it there, much to the dread of the populace who feared incurring the wrath of the gods if they moved it.

In 1146, Taira Kiyomori led a number of samurai in a skirmish with some sohei who were carrying a mikoshi. In true samurai manner, he refused to be cowed by any opponent, divine or otherwise, and he fired an arrow at the shrine. Angry at this affront to sohei sensibilities, the Enryaku-ji sent 7000 armed monks into the streets of Kyoto and demanded that Kiyomori be punished. Well aware that the only protection the court had was from the samurai, Kiyomori was only made to pay a token fine.

During the Gempei War, the monks became involved in the power struggles between the Taira and the Minamoto clans. The period gave rise to several of the most acclaimed sohei heroes, notably Jomyo Meishu, Tajima and the ever-faithfull Benkei. Many temples and monasteries were destroyed by fire at the time, and during one battle in 1180, 3500 monks of the Kofukiji temple died in the flames. The victorious general, Taira Shigihira,

later displayed 1000 heads taken from sohei killed in the fighting.

The power of the sohei was finally broken in the 16th century. Persistent interference by sohei armies in the wars between rival clans convinced the great warlord, Oda Nobunaga, that political stability depended upon destroying the monks. In 1571, he had Mount Hiei surrounded by troops and set fire to over 3000 buildings, slaughtering any of the monks who escaped the flames.

Above: An army of sohei (warrior monks) go into battle carrying their sacred mikoshi, a portable shrine.

Emperor Go-Daigo

In 1318, Go-Daigo, the 96th emperor of Japan, ascended the throne. Unlike many of his predecessors, who were children controlled by others, Go-Daigo was 31 years old when he became emperor and was determined not to be anyone's puppet. He realised that the Hojo regents were no longer the force they used to be; Hojo Takatoki found his pleasures in sex and organising dog fights and, for many of the samurai, the shogun in Kamakura was simply a weak figurehead under the control of degenerate regents.

Go-Daigo began to exert his authority in 1321 by abolishing the practice of Insei, or 'Cloistered Government'. He set about reforming the administrative organs of his government in preparation for the day when he would wield real power in the land, creating advisory councils to help him rule efficiently. However, before he could assume full authority he had to seize power from the Hojo regents. In 1331, he rose in revolt, fleeing from Kyoto with the imperial regalia. He sought refuge in a temple on the top of Mount Kasagi, which he had fortified, and called upon his supporters for aid.

Go-Daigo's son, Prince Morinaga, was the abbot of Mount Hiei and commanded large numbers of sohei. A strong Bakufu army was sent to attack the Enryaku-ji temple as it was thought that Go-Daigo was there, and although the Enryaku-ji fell to the Hojo forces, Prince Morinaga escaped to the Akasaka fortress at Kawachi, commanded by one of Go-Daigo's most devoted supporters, Kusunoki Masashige. Go-Daigo himself was not so lucky and was taken prisoner after Kasagi was overcome by Hojo troops. In 1332, he was exiled to Oki Island and his cause seemed hopeless.

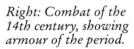

Right: Combat of the 14th century, showing armour of the period.

WARRIOR DOLLS

As he had done in the past, Kusunoki relied on surprise and unusual tactics to defend Chihaya against the huge numbers of his enemies. The 'Taiheiki' ('Chronicle of the Great Peace' — an ironically titled chronicle of the violent period between 1318-68), recounts one of the tactics he used to lower both the numbers of troops opposing him and their morale.

Kusonoki told his men to make two dozen life-sized dummies equipped with armour and weapons. During the night, they were placed behind shields near the castle walls, with a number of expert archers hidden behind them. As the sun rose, Kusunoki's warriors began to shout out their battle cries, provoking the Hojo forces to attack what they believed to be the defenders leaving the castle. The Hojo samurai advanced, each one desperate to be the first to come to grips with the enemy, but as they drew near they were met with a volley of arrows from the hidden archers, who then retreated into the castle. The attackers pressed valiantly on to the foot of the castle walls to attack the dummies.

The 'Taiheiki' tells us that Kusunoki: '...ordered his men to drop dozens of huge rocks all at one time. The rocks fell on them as they gathered near the dolls, killing over 300 soldiers and gravely wounding more than 500. When the fighting was finished, the attackers saw to their dismay that what they had taken for stalwart warriors were merely dolls. What glory could there be for their companions who had been crushed to death while attempting to attack these figures? And how ignominious were those who had been too scared to advance against such opponents!'

Left: The defence of Chihaya Castle by Kusunoki Masashige, showing the clever use of terrain that was charactersitic of his campaigns.

Fooling the Hojo

The struggle, however, was far from over. Kusunoki Masashige proved to be a warrior of singular genius. He refused to give in and harried the Hojo forces continuously, fighting a kind of guerrilla war with small numbers of men against much larger forces.

When the Hojo army attacked Kusunoki's fortress in Kawachi, he opposed them with only 500 men. His stronghold, which was actually just a wooden palisade and towers with an area of about 543 sq m (650 sq yd), contained 200 samurai, while the remaining 300 were positioned on a nearby hill, hidden by the forest. When the Bakufu troops attacked, they were subjected to very accurate archery, and those that came close to the walls had huge logs, rocks, and boiling water dropped on them. When they drew back to rest and regroup, they were attacked by the troops Kusunoki had placed on the hillsides.

Although Kusunoki's forces were proving difficult to defeat, he knew that eventually sheer weight of numbers would secure a Hojo victory. To avoid defeat, he resorted to an elaborate subterfuge. His plan was to fool the Hojo forces into believing that he was dead and the garrison all victims of seppuku. At night, he and his men slipped through the Hojo lines in small groups, leaving one man to cremate a vast pile of corpses gathered from among the slain. His ruse worked, and the Hojo were fooled into believing the emperor's supporters dead.

Kusunoki recaptured Akasaka, which he held for a month and then fell back to the fortress of Chihaya, on Mount Kongo. The Bakufu was very aware that Kusunoki's resistance was a threat and so a major attack was planned to destroy his stronghold at Chihaya. It is estimated that 100,000 troops were used to subdue Kusunoki, who opposed them with only 2000 men.

Right: A splendid lacquer inro (portable medicine box) depicting the famous occasion of Kusunoki Masashige's farewell to his son, Masatsura, before the Battle of Minatogawa.

Below right: When Kamakura fell the Hojo leaders committed a mass act of seppuku in the privacy of this cave at the rear of a temple.

Below: Nitta Yoshisada prepares to throw his sword into the sea as an offering so that the gods will roll back the tide and let his army pass.

Go-Daigo's Return

Kusunoki's audacious and successful resistance encouraged others to oppose the Hojo. Go-Daigo returned from his exile and the Bakufu decided to concentrate their main thrust on the emperor, instead of wasting men on Kusunoki.

Ashikaga Takauji, an experienced and trusted general who was descended from the Minamoto clan, was ordered to lead his troops against Go-Daigo. He realised that the confused situation could be exploited for the benefit of his family, and he changed sides, launching an attack on Kyoto on June 10, 1333. He captured the city in the emperor's name and killed the Bakufu's representatives. Kamakura itself was attacked 10 days later by another powerful samurai leader who had abandoned the Bakufu for the imperial cause: Nitta Yoshisada.

Nitta Yoshisada, whose clan was related to the Ashikaga, took the city on July 5. According to the 'Taiheiki', Yoshisada's victory depended in part upon divine assistance. To avoid a Hojo strongpoint at the Gokuraku-ji Pass, Yoshisada needed to march his troops along a beach and so turn the Hojo flank.

He prayed to Amaterasu and the Vairocana Buddha, asking that the sea might be rolled back to allow his troops easy passage and, for good measure, he threw his sword into the sea as an offering to the eight dragon gods of the oceans. His prayers were answered and the sea drew back, exposing a wide flat beach. The gods' generosity enabled Yoshisada to cross the head of the bay along the sands and approach Kamakura

from the south. The street fighting in Kamakura was savage but eventually the Hojo forces were defeated. Together with his supporters, the last of the Hojo regents killed himself and Go-Daigo regained the throne. It seemed that imperial rule had been restored to Japan. But the 'Kemmu Restoration', as Go-Daigo's rule is known, was not destined to survive; as often happened in Japanese history, a strong warrior was waiting to seize control.

The Ashikaga shoguns

Go-Daigo wanted to prevent any samurai clan from gaining enough power to dictate his policy, so, as far as he was able, he sought to rule through civilian ministers. Soon after his return to Kyoto in 1333, an office, known as the musha-dokoro, was established to control the samurai in the city.

Go-Daigo's plans did not find a willing supporter in Ashikaga Takauji. As a descendant of the Minamoto clan, Takauji saw his role as restoring and reinvigorating the office of shogun with himself in the central position, so continuing the policy established by his Minamoto ancestors. Hojo Tokiyuki, the son of the last Hojo regent, provided Takauji with the perfect opportunity to seize power when he rose up against Go-Daigo, successfully attacking and capturing Kamakura.

Takauji was appointed to punish Tokiyuki's act of rebellion, which he rapidly did, but once his forces were mobilised he proceeded to attack Nitta Yoshisada and seized his lands. Once again, a state of war existed between the imperial forces and their supporters — represented by Nitta and Kusunoki — and a powerful warlord — Ashikaga Takauji — who was identified with the interests of the samurai and the restoration of samurai government.

At first the imperial forces dominated, forcing Takauji to flee to Kyushu, but as many of the powerful samurai clans wanted a return to the shogunate, they declared for Ashikaga Takauji. On April 14, 1336, a battle at Tadara resulted in a decisive victory for the Ashikaga clan and their supporters.

Takauji and his brother, Tadayoshi, began to move their forces by land and sea towards Kyoto. They were joined by reinforcements from their allies until a formidable army was assembled. To oppose them, Nitta Yoshisada assembled an army on the banks of the River Minato.

Kusunoki's warning

Emperor Go-Daigo ordered Masashige Kusunoki to take his troops and join Yoshisada, but he advised the emperor to withdraw to Mount Hiei and avoid a battle with the Ashikaga forces, realising that they were too powerful to be defeated in a single encounter. Kusunoki's warning was ignored on the advice of Go-Daigo's courtiers, who believed that the imperial forces were strong enough to defeat the Ashikaga army.

Loyal to the emperor, Kusunoki had no choice but to obey his commands, no matter how disastrous they might prove to be. Anticipating his own death and the end of the imperial cause, Kusunoki called for his 10-year-old son, Masatsuru. He made the young boy swear an oath that if he heard of his father's death in the battle he would gather the remnants of the imperial forces and withdraw to Mount Kongo to continue the struggle.

Above: A portrait scroll of Kusunoki Masashige, the exemplar of samurai loyalty to the emperor.

Right: The last stand
of the Kusunoki clan
at the Battle of Shijo-
Nawate, in 1348.

The Ashikaga Victorious

At the Battle of Minatogawa, Kusunoki's predictions were proved correct. By the late afternoon, it was obvious that the Ashikaga had gained the victory and Kusunoki and his brother Masasue went to a nearby farmhouse to commit seppuku in the traditional manner.

Kusunoki asked his brother if he had any last wishes, to which he replied, 'I would like to be reborn seven times into this world of men so that I might destroy the enemies of the court'. Kusunoki agreed and the brothers proceeded to rip open their stomachs. Around 50 of Kusunoki's followers who had survived the battle, duly joined their lord in death by committing seppuku simultaneously.

Kusunoki's head was sent to his family so that they might look upon his features for the last time. Just as his young son Masatsuru was preparing to follow his father's example by taking his own life, he was discovered by his mother who seized his arm, saying: 'You are still young, but if you really are your father's son, how can you stray so far from your duty? If now you take your life, you will not only destroy your father's name but fail in your duty to His Majesty'.

Ashikaga Takauji entered Kyoto on July 8, 1336, to find that Go-Daigo had fled to seek sanctuary and support from the warrior monks of Mount Hiei. Takauji selected an imperial prince and installed him as Emperor Komyo. Go-Daigo left Mount Hiei and was taken into custody by Ashikaga Takauji. He was made to surrender the imperial regalia to Komyo but, according to contemporary witnesses, the regalia that he surrendered were imitations.

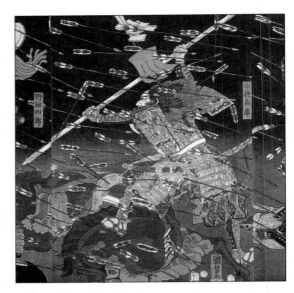

The two courts

In January 1337, Go-Daigo escaped from Kyoto and set up court at Yoshino, south of Nara. From 1337 until 1392, Japan was ruled by two emperors. The legitimate line in Yoshino was known as the Southern Court; the Northern Court sat in Kyoto and was controlled by a succession of Ashikaga shoguns. The period of the two courts is known as the Nambokucho.

The struggle between the two imperial lines was marked by constant war as powerful landowners, generals, factions of the imperial family, and various members of the shogunate, squabbled and fought for dominance. Kusunoki Masatsuru fulfilled his obligation to his father by becoming the commander of the Southern Court's army in 1347, as a follower of Go-Daigo's

Below: Ashikaga
Takauji, the first
Ashikaga shogun,
holds court in his
capital of Kyoto.

THE ONIN WAR

The Onin War (so-called because it began in the first year of the 'Onin' year-period) began as a dispute between the two most powerful samurai families in Kyoto: the Yamana and the Hosokawa. Hostilities were brought to a head by a disputed succession within the ruling family. Shogun Ashikaga Yoshimasa abdicated his position, appointing his brother, Yoshimi, as his heir. His wife later bore him a son, Yoshihisa, whom she claimed was the rightful heir. The Yamana supported Yoshihisa, while the Hosowaka backed Yoshimi.

Soon each clan had begun to concentrate its troops in Kyoto. Fighting began at the end of May 1467, and by July, a sizable section of Kyoto was in ruins. The Onin War saw the emergence of a new kind of warrior: the ashigaru (light-feet). The ashigaru were often from peasant backgrounds and were armed with naginata and spears, and equipped with light armour.

The war ended in 1477 with no clear victor. Although the Ashikaga shoguns continued to hold office until 1597, the end of the war saw the military power of the shogun in eclipse. Like the emperor, the office of shogun was respected as a symbol, but real power lay in the hands of the powerful new warlords who emerged from the chaos of the Sengoku Jidai — the 'Age of the Country at War'.

Left: Ashikaga Yoshimasa was an aesthete rather than a statesman, responsible for the building of the Silver Pavillion in Kyoto, but also for the disastrous Onin War.

successor, Go-Murakami. He met his death on February 4, 1348, fighting the Ashikaga at Shijo, Nawate, along with other members of his family.

The war became a struggle for land, and the old samurai virtues of loyalty and duty, exemplified by Kusunoki Masashige, were eroded to some extent as clans and individuals frequently changed sides to gain some advantage. Fighting was chaotic and confused; Kyoto was conquered four times between 1353 and 1355, as various groups gained a temporary advantage only to lose it as new alliances emerged.

In 1392, the two imperial lines merged when the third Ashikaga shogun, Yoshimitsu, persuaded the Southern Court to return to Kyoto and agree to a settlement by which the succession was to alternate between the two lines. In fact, the terms of the settlement were never met and the claims of Go-Daigo's descendants have persisted, unsuccessfully, into modern times. After World War II, 17 claimants to the throne appealed to the Occupation Forces to restore them to their rightful position.

Peasant uprisings

The country gradually sank into anarchy and, although no major wars were fought in the first half of the 15th century, this period saw widespread agrarian unrest as the peasants organised themselves into ikki (or armed leagues) for self-protection.

The Ashikaga Bakufu was not strong enough to protect the peasants from attack or to redress their grievances. Instead, the peasants looked to samurai who had become farmers, or to dispossessed samurai, for leadership. The policy of the ikki was simple: they rioted and attacked pawnbrokers and moneylenders. In 1441, Kyoto was severely damaged after a week of rioting and looting, and in 1457 the ikki defeated a Bakufu army of around 800 samurai.

Below: The gap between the classes in Japan was not always as wide as is commonly supposed. This samurai house, though large, is built of the same materials as used for a peasant's cottage.

'The Age of the Country at War'

Right: A fine suit of armour from the Museo Stibbert in Florence, having unusual solid plate sode (shoulder guards).

Below: A group of archers dressed for a performance of the mounted martial art of yabusame, which involved shooting small targets from the back of a horse.

The Years of Struggle

The end of the Onin War in 1477 left a political vacuum, with no strong figure at the centre able to impose his will on the course of events. It was inevitable that many warriors would seize such an opportunity to enlarge their land holdings. This age is known to Japanese historians as the Sengoku Jidai: 'The Age of the Country at War'.

The name was taken from a period in Chinese history (403-222 BC) known as the Warring States, which preceded the unification of China by the Ch'in dynasty. The name was well chosen. For almost 150 years, Japan was wracked by almost constant fighting between the armies of powerful samurai lords, religious groups and warrior monks.

Piracy and raids on the Chinese mainland increased to the point where the Chinese government was forced to appoint General Ch'i Chi-kuang to suppress the raids. Between 1559 and 1567, his troops took 21,500 heads of

Japanese raiders and their Chinese helpers. Ch'i Chi-kuang described the Japanese warriors he faced: 'The numerous battles I have fought over the past several years give me the impression that the pirates always manage to sit on the heights waiting for us. Usually they hold on until evening, when our soldiers become tired, then they dash out. Or else, when we start to withdraw, they catch us out of step to launch their counter-attack.

'It seems that they always manage to send forth their units when they are fresh and spirited. They adorn their helmets with coloured strings and animal horns of metallic colours and ghostly shapes to frighten our soldiers. Many of them carry mirrors; their spears and swords are polished to a shine and look dazzling under the sun. Our soldiers are awed by them during the hours of delay before contact'.

THE ASAKURA HOUSE LAWS

It was quite common for daimyo of the time to write their own Kaho, or House Laws, laying down rules to be followed by their followers and descendants in order that the domain should be preserved. Asakura Toshikage (1428-81) left a code of 17 articles, the 'Toshikage Jushichikajo', a fascinating document which reflects many of the ideas and practices of the newly emerged daimyo. Toshikage's laws included the following recommendations:

'1. In the fief of the Asakura, one should not determine hereditary chief retainers. A man should be assigned according to his ability and loyalty....

3. One should place spies in fiefs near and far, even in times of peace, and should constantly inquire into their circumstances....

4. One should not be overly fond of famous swords and daggers. Even if one has a sword valued at 10,000 cash, he will not overcome 100 men carrying spears valued at 100 cash. Therefore if one has 10,000 cash and buys 100 spears, having 100 men to carry them he should be able to protect an entire flank....

15. It should be strictly forbidden to construct in our provinces, any castle other than the one [Ichijogatani] held by the Asakura family. All men of high rank should be constantly maintained at Ichijogatani, and only their representatives and underlings should be placed in their home areas'.

Left: The concealment of a bladed weapon within the neck of a seemingly harmless biwa (a type of lute) shows the lengths to which samurai of the Sengoku Jidai could go to overcome their enemies by deceit and treachery.

The sengoku daimyo

Many of the large landowners under the Ashikaga shoguns held their lands as grants or awards for service from the shogunate. Known as shugo daimyo, they were appointed by the shogun to govern a particular area and to administer the laws of the shogunate.

Inevitably, most of them used their official posts to strengthen their own positions, acquiring land by any means available, including war. In order to exert some degree of control over the shugo daimyo, it became a standard policy of the Ashikaga shoguns to insist that they reside near to the shogun in Kyoto, leaving deputies to administer their fiefs.

With the collapse of the Ashikaga Bakufu, a new breed of daimyo emerged; powerful regional rulers who had no interest in appealing to any kind of central authority. These were the sengoku daimyo: men — often from relatively humble backgrounds — who held no shogunal commissions, but whose authority depended on how much military power they could directly control.

The sengoku daimyo were, to all intents and purposes, independent rulers of autonomous states, whose strength and security depended on their own efforts. Japanese writers describing the conditions of the time often use the term gekokujo (the low oppress the high), indicating the scale of the changes.

The Changing Domains

The domains controlled by the daimyo grew more cohesive as it became impossible to defend widely scattered land-holdings. The old shoen estates disappeared and the old feudal relationships between lord and retainer were re-established, with warriors owing direct allegiance to their daimyo.

The daimyo's authority was based on his ability to wage war, rather than the sanction of a central power. So, to meet the cost of wars, the sengoku daimyo concentrated their energies on increasing their wealth. The land itself became better governed and new land was brought into cultivation as the daimyo attempted to improve their economic base. Wherever possible, trade with China was expanded and developed. One valued export was weapons; in 1483, 37,000 sword and naginata blades were sent to China in return for porcelain, iron, copper coins, silks, books and medicines.

Below: A scene from the annual archery contest held at the Sanjusangendo Temple in Kyoto.

If precious metals were discovered on a daimyo's lands, deep mines were sunk to extract the ore, and the gold and silver was used to strengthen the economic power of the fief. One side benefit was the development of skilled miners, whose talents could be used by a daimyo to undermine the walls of an enemy castle during a siege.

As daimyo improved the government and economy of their domains, towns grew up around the castles they had built to serve as administrative and military centres. The increased efficiency and administrative skill of the daimyo also encompassed the peasants living in the domains, who were now eligible for military service. Armed with spears and pikes and protected by light armour, the disciplined groups of peasant ashigaru changed the face of war. The mounted samurai fighting for his own glory was replaced by an officer who obeyed orders and directed the movements of massed infantry.

Military specialists

Constant warfare meant that anyone with specialist military knowledge was highly valued by the daimyo. Experts in strategy and tactics, known as gunpaisha because of the large fan-like metal gunpai they carried, were employed by the daimyo to direct their troops.

The use of spies, metsuke (eye-attachers), was widespread and assassination was an accepted method of removing a dangerous enemy. To prevent an enemy from infiltrating spies into a domain, all movements between the domains were carefully scrutinised and expert spy-catchers, known as meakashi (eye-clearers), were employed by some daimyo to ferret out enemy agents.

Ruthless tactics were used to place agents in enemy territory. At the end of the 16th century, it is said that Hojo Soun employed a number of blind people as spies. To enable his agents to pose as refugees, he announced that any blind people living in his territory were of no value, and had all those living in the immediate vicinity of his castle town rounded up and thrown into the sea. The remaining blind people in his domain naturally sought protection from neighbouring daimyo, where some of them spied for their lord.

Expert martial artists were particularly valued by the daimyo as instructors for their samurai. Ryu (schools of martial techniques) were established by master swordsmen to promote their particular style of fighting. The inner secrets of the ryu were only taught to the most dedicated students, who followed the master's teaching unquestioningly.

The first ryu that can be reliably dated is the Tenshin Shoden Shinto Ryu, founded by Iezasu Choisai Ienao (1387-1488). He spent his early years in the service of the Ashikaga family

SWORD TESTING

The arts of a master swordsman counted for little if he could not rely on his blade for strength and cutting power. To ensure a sword's reliability, the newly finished blade was sometimes given to a professional sword tester.

The sword tester's 'craft' was among the most brutal aspects of the samurai past, testing the cutting power of a new sword on corpses taken from the execution grounds, and sometimes the living bodies of condemned criminals. Twenty different cuts were used, beginning with severing the hand by cutting through the wrist, and progressing through the thicker limbs of the body.

The results of the test were usually recorded on the nakago (sword tang — the piece of metal attaching the sword to the handle), and it is not uncommon to find inscriptions on old swords giving details such as 'two men cut' or 'eight arms severed'.

Samurai swords were capable of slicing through tremendous resistance. Several 17th century blades bear the inscription 'mitsudo setsudan' (three bodies with one cut). In the martial art of iai-jutsu (the art of drawing the sword) one of the techniques taught is cutting the body in two by slicing through the torso from the right hip to the left shoulder.

Below: Final touches being applied at a sword polisher's establishment.

and then founded his school of swordsmanship. Other master swordsmen followed his example, and warriors well-versed in the skills of a ryu were highly prized by the daimyo. The incessant fighting during the Sengoku Jidai meant that swordsmen had many opportunities to test their skills. Those who survived were indeed masters of their art, and observing the lessons they taught could make a decisive difference in combat.

Left: A general urges his troops into battle by waving his warfan.

THE SOUL OF THE SAMURAI

O f all the weapons in the samurai's arsenal, the sword was the most important and the most closely identified with the warrior class. The sword was more than just an implement for combat; it had a symbolic value as the repository of the samurai's honour. As Tokugawa Ieyasu said, 'the sword is the soul of the samurai'.

Casual treatment of a blade was taken as an insult to the owner and could have lethal consequences. Accordingly, a highly detailed etiquette evolved around the correct way to wear, touch and use the traditional sword of the Japanese warrior, which is still followed by practitioners of traditional martial arts.

The samurai normally wore two swords, known as daisho (long/short), the longer weapon, or daito, being over 60 cm (24 in) in length, and the shorter weapon, or wakizashi, being between 30 to 60 cm (12 to 24 in). Longer swords (no daichi) were also made: one no dachi associated with Hojo Tokimune was 1.77 m long (5.8 ft). In battle, they were carried or worn slung across the back.

The samurai often valued their swords above all other things. Akechi Mitsuhide — the samurai who murdered the ruler of Japan, Oda Nobunaga, in 1582 — provided a good example of the samurai's attachment to their weapons when besieged in his castle by Hori Hidemasa. Facing certain death, his first concern was that his swords should survive intact and he sent a message to Hidemasa, saying: 'I have many excellent swords, which I have cherished all of my life... they are part of the heritage of Japan itself. I will die happy, if you will stop your attack for a short while, so that I can have the swords sent out'. Hidemasa agreed and the weapons were lowered from the castle walls, carefully wrapped in padding to protect them.

Swords were often given names and it was believed that some weapons were particularly lucky or malevolent. One master swordsmith, Muramasa, was famous for the quality of his blades, but as he was mentally unstable it was thought that his blades were blood-thirsty and would bring bad luck to their owners. One owner, seeking to test his Muramasa blade, placed it in a stream as some dead leaves floated past. Each leaf that touched the edge was sliced in two. A blade by Japan's greatest swordsmith, Masamune, was then placed in the stream; the leaves swirled around the blade but avoided the edge.

Below: Two swords of the tachi style, carried with the cutting edge downwards.

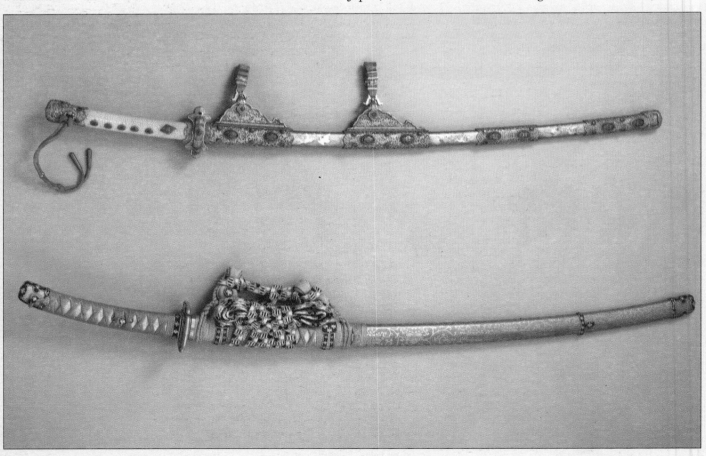

The swordsmith's art

Swordsmiths in all countries have been faced with the same basic problem: how to create a weapon combining the optimum toughness and sharpness. Iron combined with carbon at a high temperature and allowed to cool slowly, produces a blade that is hard to break but will not take a very sharp edge. If the metal is cooled quickly, by being plunged into cold water, it is possible to make a sharp blade that is very hard but has little tensile strength. The swordsmith's quest was to produce a weapon that combined strength and flexibility in the correct proportions.

The oldest swords found in Japan were straight thrusting weapons, similar to examples found in China. According to tradition, the first native Japanese blade was made by the swordsmith Amakuni in Yamato, around AD 700. Amakuni and his son, Amakura, were employed by the emperor to make weapons for his warriors. Legend has it that Amakuni incurred the emperor's disapproval when weapons he had forged snapped during the heat of battle. Amakuni determined to forge a sword that would not break, and so regain the emperor's favour.

He and his son locked themselves in their forge and prayed to the Shinto gods for seven days and nights. Then they set to work. After a month, they emerged with a sword that curved slightly and had only one edge. Pleased with their first effort, they refined the process, and when the warriors returned from their battles the following year, none of the swords had

been broken. The methods followed by the legendary Amakuni were improved upon over the next ten centuries, but the basic technique of forging the blade remained the same. Small pieces of steel formed in a blast furnace were selected and stacked on an iron plate. This was heated in a furnace and then welded into a solid block on an anvil by pounding the metal with heavy hammers.

The block was then folded and beaten out again, repeatedly, until thousands of laminations were produced and much of the carbon in the original piece of metal was removed. Next, the block was wrapped around a strip of high carbon steel, which would produce the edge of the sword.

In the final forging, the blade was covered with a paste made of clay, charcoal, powdered grinding stone and other material, which was removed from the edge to leave a pattern typical of the smith's tradition.

The sword was heated until, in the words of one swordsmith, 'it turns to the colour of the moon about to set out on its journey across the heavens on a June or July evening', and then plunged, edge down, into water of a specified temperature.

The unprotected edge of the blade cooled quickly, while the clay covering allowed the rest of the blade to cool more slowly and so retain its flexibility. Finally, the smith signed his name on the tang and the blade was passed on to specialist craftsmen to be polished and fitted with the hilt, guard (tsuba) and other items of sword furniture.

Above: Swordsmiths at work, showing the full complex process from forging through to choosing fitments for the blade and the scabbard.

Tsukahara Bokuden

One of the most celebrated swordsmen in Japanese history was born in December 1490, at Kashima, Hitachi province, and was given the name of Takamoto. His father, a vassal of the Kashima daimyo, taught his son the art of swordsmanship from a very early age, and even as a young child Takamoto seemed to have a natural talent for the art. His skills were further increased when he was adopted by Tsukahara Tosonokami Yasumoto, a relative of the daimyo of Kashima, who recognised a potential fencer of genius in the young boy.

Takamoto's adopted father was a practitioner of the Shinto Ryu, a style that had been established by Iezasu Choisai Ienao, and soon the boy began to incorporate that system into his repertoire. The young Takamoto was determined to become the greatest swordsman in Japan, and at the age of ten he visited the Kashima shrine and asked the gods for help in achieving his ambition. While other children played, Takamoto trained with his sword in the countryside and in the precincts of the Kashima shrine. His precocious dedication paid off and by the age of 20, Takamoto was ready

to fight his first duel, challenging the famous Kyoto swordsman, Ochiai Torazaemon.

It was an ambitious challenge for such a young swordsman; and yet, for all his skill, Ochiai was no match for Takamoto, who defeated him in seconds but spared his life. Humiliation at the hands of an untried youth was too much for Ochiai and he tried to get his revenge by waiting in ambush to launch a surprise attack on Takamoto. Once again, Takamoto's skill was too great and in this encounter Ochiai lost his life as well as his reputation.

The quest for knowledge

Impressed by this demonstration of his abilities, many daimyo were eager to employ Takamoto as an instructor, but he refused them all, choosing instead to concentrate on developing his own skills. Takamoto was never too proud to learn. During his life he embarked on three musha shugyo (warrior pilgrimages) to challenge skilled swordsmen and he studied fencing from all the teachers he could find.

By the age of 37, he had established his own ryu and changed his name to Tsukahara Bokuden Takamoto (he was more usually

Below: Tsukahara Bokuden on the course of his warrior pilgrimage, designed to find suitable opponents to test his skill.

known as Tsukahara Bokuden). Like any other retainer, Bokuden was expected to fight for his lord when called upon. He was involved in 39 separate fights, including 19 bouts of single combat, where his speciality of engaging enemy commanders in combat and then killing them gained him great fame.

The single-cut style

For the medieval swordmaster, fame bore a high price. Bokuden was often challenged by other swordsmen eager to test his skill and improve their own reputations by defeating or killing him. One particularly dangerous challenge came from Kajiwara Nagato, a master of the naginata. Nagato had never been defeated in combat and was so skillful that it was said he could cut a swallow in flight.

Bokuden's followers were troubled by the challenge, believing that this time their master had met his match and might be killed, but Bokuden told them not to worry; he was confident that he could defeat Nagato. The duel took place in a field in Kawagoe, Musashi province. As Nagato stepped forward and raised his naginata, Bokuden simply stepped forward and killed him with a single cut.

This was the essence of Bokuden's style, the hitotsu-tachi (single-cut style). One of Bokuden's followers explained his approach in the following terms: 'A sword can be divided into three spheres. The first is the time of the heavens; the second, the advantage of the earth; the third, the combination of the earth and the heavens. This is the secret of hitotsu-tachi'.

Bokuden's reputation grew and he was appointed instructor to Shogun Ashikaga Yoshiteru, the most prestigious position in the land. Unfortunately for the shogun, even

Bokuden's skills could not prevent Yoshiteru from being murdered in 1565 by rebel vassals of the Hosokawa family.

Above: An excellent illustration of swordfighting, showing the sleeves tied back using a cord, and the hakama (trousers) hitched up through the belt.

Left: The assassination of Shogun Ashikaga Yoshiteru, patron of Tsukahara Bokuden.

The No-Sword School

By the time he reached the age of 50, Bokuden had achieved all of his ambitions. He no longer felt the need to prove his abilities and would refuse to engage in combat for its own sake. A famous story about Bokuden is often used by modern-day ken-jutsu (swordsmanship) masters to illustrate the ultimate goal of the martial arts: that is, to achieve victory without causing unnecessary bloodshed.

Bokuden was travelling on a ferry across Lake Biwa with a number of other passengers. One of the passengers was a particularly arrogant and aggressive samurai, who continually boasted of his skill with the sword, saying that no one in Japan could equal his ability. Bokuden sat quietly ignoring the braggart, a response which naturally infuriated the samurai. Trying to pick a fight with Bokuden, the samurai asked him if he knew anything about swordsmanship.

Bokuden said: 'My art is different from yours. It consists not so much in defeating others but in not being defeated'.

'What is the name of your school?' demanded the samurai.

'The Mutekatsu Ryu,' replied Bokuden. This made the samurai even more angry, since the name means 'to defeat an enemy without hands' — that is, without a sword.

Below: The title of this print tells us that it depicts the aged Tsukahara Bokuden teaching sword-fighting to the young Miyamoto Musashi. Musashi was in fact born 12 years after Bokuden's death, so the incident is fictitious. Bokuden receives the blows from Musashi's wooden swords on the lid of a rice pot.

'What nonsense is this,' shouted the samurai. He told the boatman to land on a small island where Bokuden could display his art in a match with himself.

As the boat drew up to the beach, the samurai leaped out and drew his sword. Bokuden slowly stood up and picked up the boatman's pole, saying, 'I do not need a sword'. He put the pole into the water and with a strong push moved the boat into deep water, abandoning the samurai on the beach. Smiling, Bokuden said to the samurai, 'Here is my no-sword school'.

Bokuden's test

Bokuden's emphasis on a disciplined approach to ken-jutsu extended to his own family. He had three adopted sons who all received training in the use of the sword. Desiring to test their ability, he once placed a block of wood above the entrance to his room, arranged so that it should fall on anyone entering. He then called for his eldest son who, sensing that something was wrong, caught the wooden block as he walked through the door. Bokuden nodded approvingly and called for the second son, who avoided the falling block, reaching for his sword as he did so.

Bokuden then called for the third son, who walked into the room and cut the block of wood in half as it fell, with a lightning-fast

THE SINGLE-MINDED LEAGUE

The Jodo-Shinshu is an offshoot of the Jodo (Pure Land) sect of Buddhism. Founded in the 12th century by a Buddhist monk called Honen (1133-1212), Jodo teaches that salvation may be obtained by calling on the name of the Amida Buddha. This approach, concentrating on faith rather than on the intellect or meditation, received much popular support, and the various Jodo sects attracted many followers.

In the 15th century, a Jodo preacher called Rennyo (1415-99) managed to unify many of the sects into a new group, known as the Ikko-ikki (Single-Minded League). The league proved particularly successful at attracting new members. It was initially organised along very egalitarian principles and its members were permitted to marry. Moreover, the Ikko-ikki taught that death in battle meant salvation, a doctrine which helped to make the Ikko-ikki a formidable military force.

By 1488, the league had ejected Togashi Masachika, the daimyo of Kaga, from his domains and taken over the province, which they continued to hold until 1580. They built a massive fortification, the Ishiyama Hongan-ji, at the mouth of the River Yodo, which became their military base and the centre of their religion. By 1520, the Ikko-ikki controlled three provinces and had at their disposal a huge army, as powerful and effective as any daimyo's. Looking for plunder, they turned their attentions to Kyoto and, in 1528, their army approached the city.

Kyoto was the stronghold of another Buddhist sect, the Hokke-shu (Lotus sect), who followed the teachings of Nichiren. Kyoto was an important centre of the faith, with 21 temples in the city. Faced by the approaching Ikko-ikki, the shogun, Ashikaga Yoshiharu, fled, but the followers of the Hokke-shu mobilised their forces and raised a huge army that drove off the Ikko-ikki.

In 1533, the Lotus army formed an alliance with Hosokawa Harumoto and attacked the Ikko-ikki's stronghold of the Ishiyama Hongan-ji. Although the fortress did not fall, Kyoto was made effectively safe from attack, thereby enabling the shogun to return to the capital city.

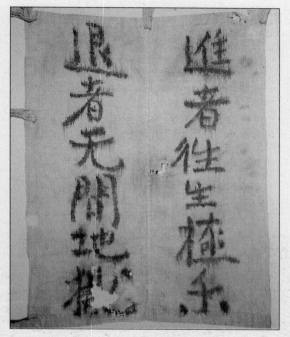

Left: The flag of the Ikko-ikki, bearing an inscription which reads, 'He who advances is sure of heaven, but he who retreats will suffer eternal damnation'.

slash of his sword. While the youngest son had displayed tremendous technique, Bokuden decided that his eldest son's response had shown that he should become the next head of his ryu, as he had achieved victory without drawing his blade.

In 1571, Bokuden died. His ryu did not survive without him as most of his senior students died in the many battles that occurred at that time. His most trusted disciple, Kitabatake Tomonori, met his death fighting the armies of the famous warlord Oda Nobunaga, and with his death the secret of Bokuden's style vanished.

However, part of his message was preserved in the 'Bokuden Hyakushu', a collection of 98 poems ascribed to Bokuden. These teach that a samurai should try to achieve composure at the line which separates life from death, an ideal which many samurai have searched for since.

Left: Lake Biwa, scene of one of Bokuden's most famous challenges.

The Warlords

Of all the daimyo that fought for dominance during the Sengoku Jidai, two of the most powerful were Uesugi Kenshin (1530-78) and Takeda Shingen (1521-73). Uesugi Kenshin was adopted into the Uesugi family in 1551 when he provided refuge for Uesugi Norimasa after his defeat at the hands of the Hojo clan. Norimasa made his former vassal his son and heir and gave him the title of Lord of Echigo province and head of the Uesugi clan.

His great opponent, Takeda Shingen, achieved his position in true sengoku style, by rising in revolt against his father in 1540 when he discovered that he was about to be disinherited in favour of a younger brother. He seized control of the Takeda domain and ruled it efficiently, providing security for the farmers and establishing a powerful army. His expansionist policy brought him into conflict with Uesugi Kenshin, whose lands bordered on those of the Takeda.

Between 1553 and 1564, they fought five battles at Kawanakajima, without either side dominating. At the fourth battle, in 1561, Takeda Shingen and one of his generals, Yamamoto Kansuke, devised a plan by which Uesugi's forces would be caught and destroyed in a surprise pincer movement. Due to Uesugi's vigilance, the plan failed and during the fierce

hand-to-hand fighting, Takeda Nobushige, Shingen's younger brother, was killed.

Yamamoto Kansuke, who was aged 70, blamed himself for the failure of the surprise attack and decided that the only way to make amends to Takeda Shingen was to die in battle. Picking up a spear, he charged into the mass of the Uesugi samurai and fought with great courage until, overcome by bullet wounds, he committed seppuku on a nearby hill.

Takeda Shingen sat in his headquarters, sending commands to his troops via his tsukai-ban (messenger corps), who were identified by a sashimono (banner) which bore the device of a running centipede. Although under pressure, the Takeda samurai were fighting well, but some of Uesugi's warriors managed to get close to the Takeda headquarters and engaged Takeda Shingen's bodyguard in combat.

As they did so, a single mounted samurai, wearing a white cowl and a green surcoat over his armour, burst in and attacked Shingen with a sword. It was Uesugi Kenshin who had come to fight his opponent, man-to-man. Shingen could not draw his sword and so he blocked Uesugi's blows with his heavy war fan. He took three blows on his armour and seven on the fan until one of his retainers, Hara Osumi-no-kami, attacked Uesugi with a spear. The spear slid off Uesugi's armour and hit his horse, making it rear up. The pause in the proceedings

Below: The army of Takeda Shingen, encamped ready for one of the several battles at Kawanakajima, receives intelligence from Yamamoto Kansuke, who kneels before Shingen.

THE FIRST GUNS

In 1542 or 1543, the date is uncertain, a Chinese junk was caught in a storm and blown onto the shores of the island of Tanegashima, off the coast of southern Kyushu. On board were three Portuguese travellers who became the first Westerners to land on Japanese soil.

Their strange clothes and appearance attracted interest, but what really caught the attention of the Japanese were the guns that two of them carried. Lord Tokitada, the daimyo of Tanegashima, saw one of the Portuguese shoot a duck. Impressed with the power of this new weapon, he arranged for shooting lessons and within one month he had bought both guns for 1000 taels of gold each.

Drawing upon the metalworking skills of his swordsmith, Yatsuita Kinbei, Tokitada told him to make copies of the guns. Tradition recounts that making the barrels was straightforward enough, but cutting a screw thread for the breech plug was beyond the swordsmith's skills until he learned the secret from a Portuguese armourer who arrived in a ship a few months later. Yatsuida paid a high price for the secret; the captain of the ship took his 17-year-old daughter in payment.

Yatsuita produced a large number of copies, which Lord Tokitada traded. Within 10 years, the new weapons were being manufactured to a high standard all over Japan and they began to appear on the battlefield. The gun appealed to military leaders for a number of reasons. It could be produced quickly and relatively cheaply, and infantry could be drilled in a short time to a high level of efficiency, so making the ashigaru equal to the best of the samurai.

One of the few samurai to understand the potential of the new weapon was Takeda Shingen. In 1571, he told his commanders: 'Hereafter, guns will be the most important weapons. Therefore, decrease the number of spears [in your armies] and have the most capable men carry guns'. Ironically, Shingen died from a gunshot wound in April 1573.

Left: Japanese carrying guns, as seen by a Dutch artist who met the first Japanese to reach Manila.

gave Shingen's personal guards time to intervene to save their lord and drive Uesugi Kenshin away.

This combat between two of the most powerful Sengoku Jidai warlords is famous in samurai history (it has been the inspiration for numerous woodblock prints) and illustrates the fact that, although warfare had become more organised, involving large bodies of infantry and cavalry moving in formation, the spirit of the lone warrior, fighting his enemy face-to-face, had not entirely disappeared.

At the end of the fighting, it was considered that the Takeda forces were the victors, although in fact both sides had been severely mauled. Takeda Shingen held a head-viewing ceremony, during which 3117 enemy heads were exhibited.

Storming the Castle

At the end of the 1550s, Takeda Shingen formed an alliance with the Hojo clan in order to conquer all the Uesugi castles in the province of Kozuke. In 1561, the Takeda troops arrived at the fortress of Minowa, defended by a retainer of the Uesugi, Nagano Narimori. His father, Narimasa, had just died and the Takeda forces believed that the castle would fall easily. However, the son proved as able as the father and was supported by a warrior of great ability, Kamiizumi Hidetsuna.

Shingen wanted to subdue the castle quickly, and so he decided against a long siege. This of course meant that the only way to take the castle was by storming the defences with his samurai, who he was confident would succeed in a short time. But the defenders put up fierce resistance and held back the Takeda forces. Wherever the fighting was at its most ferocious, a group of spearmen would appear and drive off the attackers, and it was only when Nagano Nagamori was killed that the defenders sued for peace.

Shingen was so struck by the courage and skill of the samurai who had led the spear detachment that he ordered him to be brought before him. The warrior announced himself: 'I am Kamiizumi Hidetsuna, captain of the 16 spears of Nagano, son of Kamiizumi Noritsuna, and a student of the Kage style of the martial arts'.

Impressed by Hidetsuna's skills and bearing, Shingen asked him to join his forces, but Hidetsuna declined, explaining that he wanted to dedicate himself to developing his skills with the sword and to founding a new sword school of ken-jutsu. Shingen reluctantly accepted that Hidetsuna had his own plans, but before he left, the great warlord granted Hidetsuna the right to use one of the characters from his own name. Another way of reading the character 'shin' in Shingen is 'nobu', and from this time the swordmaster was known as Kamiizumi Nobutsuna. In time, the new name became famous as the creator of one of the most famous styles of fencing in Japan: the Shinkage Ryu.

The best of enemies

Although they were enemies, Uesugi Kenshin and Takeda Shingen seem to have respected and admired one another. During one of the struggles at Kawanakajima, the head of the Hojo clan cut off Shingen's salt supply. Shingen's domains lay in the mountains, so he could not easily obtain access to the sea to procure a ready supply of salt.

As soon as Kenshin heard of Shingen's predicament, he sent some salt to Shingen from his own province, which lay on the coast of the

THE WARRIOR PHILOSOPHER

Takeda Shingen's skill as a warrior was matched by his ability as a ruler. Unlike many powerful generals, he did not have a central stronghold, stating that 'my castle is in the hearts of my people', and it seems that he was a popular and just ruler, known to the farmers in his domains as 'Shingen-Ko' ('Prince Shingen').

He took the name Shingen in 1551, when he became a lay monk of Zen Buddhism, an unlikely calling for a warrior, but an aspect of his character which he seems to have taken seriously. One of his followers, Kosaka Masanobu, recorded Shingen's talks in his work, the 'Koyogunkan'.

In Chapter 40, known as the 'Iwamizudera Monogatari' ('Tale of the Iwamizu Temple'), Shingen says: 'Learning is to a man as the leaves and branches are to a tree, and it can be said that he should not be without it. Learning is not only reading books, however, but is rather something that we study to integrate with our own way of life

'One who was born into the house of a warrior, regardless of his rank or class, first acquaints himself with a man of military feats and achievements in loyalty, and, in listening to just one of his dictums each day, will in a month know 30 precepts. Needless to say, if in a year he learns 300 precepts, at the end of that time he will be much the better.

'Thus, a man can divide his mind into three parts: he should throw out those thoughts that are evil, take up those ideas that are good, and become intimate with his own wisdom.... I would honour and call wise the man who penetrates this principle, though he lacks the knowledge of a single Chinese character. As for those who are learned in other matters, I would avoid them regardless of how deep their knowledge might be. That is how shallow and untalented this monk is'.

Below: Every daimyo had an élite corps of senior retainers, who were usually family members. Here are the '24 Generals' of the Takeda clan, who served Takeda Shingen.

Sea of Japan, explaining that: 'I do not fight with salt but with the sword'.

In April 1573, Shingen was shot in the head by an enemy sentry while laying siege to Noda Castle — a fortress held by a supporter of Tokugawa Ieyasu, the man destined to rule Japan. It is said that when Kenshin heard of Shingen's death, he wept at the loss of the 'best of enemies'.

Uesugi Kenshin died in 1578. Officially, he died from an apoplectic fit whilst in the lavatory. However, there is a tradition that a ninja had hidden in the cess pit under the toilet and killed him with a thrust of his spear; a grisly tale, but not one with much historical foundation. Medical evidence suggests that Kenshin suffered from stomach cancer and died from the effects of a stroke.

The Path to Unification

Oda Nobunaga

Three men were responsible for ending the
chaos of the Sengoku Jidai and setting Japan on
the path to unification. Oda Nobunaga (1534-
82) came from a small fief in Owari province,
and, like many of the sengoku daimyo, rose to
power because of his military ability. By 1559,
he had defeated most of his neighbours and
taken control of most of the province.

One of his followers was Toyotomi
Hideyoshi, a warrior who joined Nobunaga's
army in 1558 as a low-ranking ashigaru, and
rose to high rank due to his ability. One of Oda
Nobunaga's enemies was Imagawa Yoshimoto,
who had a retainer named Tokugawa Ieyasu. In
1560, Nobunaga, with 2000 troops, defeated
Imagawa Yoshimoto at the Battle of
Okehazama by ambushing Imagawa's much

larger force of 40,000 men during a storm.
Imagawa's death in the battle released
Tokugawa Ieyasu from his obligations to his
lord and he joined Nobunaga in 1561. The
three men directly responsible for unifying
Japan were now together and their struggle for
power began.

Nobunaga prepared the way, not by using
his samurai but by a gentler form of diplomacy:
marriage. He secured the support of the Takeda
clan by marrying his daughter to Takeda
Shingen's son; he married off his sister to Asai
Nagamasa, the ruler of northern Omi.
Nobunaga himself married the daughter of
Saito Toshimasa, the lord of Mino, a man
famous for his cruelty, who took particular
delight in boiling his enemies to death. In 1556,
Saito Toshimasa's son, Yoshitatsu, killed his
father and took his place, which justified
Nobunaga in attacking Yoshitatsu to revenge
his father-in-law. However, Yoshitatsu died of
leprosy and the Saito were finally beaten by
Toyotomi Hideyoshi in 1564.

The murdered shogun

The stage was set and Nobunaga waited for the opportunity to achieve his ambition: the establishment of a single powerful government, with himself at the centre. In 1567, events gave Nobunaga the excuse he needed to act.

The post of shogun was still held by the Ashikaga family and while their power, like the emperor's, was primarily symbolic, Nobunaga realised that if he could gain control of the holder of the office of shogun, he could use this power to justify any acts of aggression. In 1545, the 13th Ashikaga shogun, Yoshiteru, became shogun at the age of 11. Yoshiteru was controlled by two men, Miyoshi Chokei and Matsunaga Hisahide, and, in 1565, these two men had Yoshiteru killed, together with his mother and his wife, and replaced him with one of his cousins.

Yoshiteru's younger brother, Yoshiaki, fled to Oda Nobunaga for protection. As in the past, when various contenders for power would have their own imperial prince to legitimise their attempts to usurp the power of the government, Nobunaga now had control of his own shogunal puppet. In 1568, he established his headquarters in the castle of Inabayama, which he renamed Gifu. The castle had been the stronghold of the Saito clan, and was taken by Nobunaga's able young general, Toyotomi Hideyoshi, in 1564.

After waging a short campaign against opposition forces in the province of Ise, Nobunaga's forces entered Kyoto and named Yoshiaki as the 15th Ashikaga shogun on December 28, 1568. Whatever prestige was left to the office of shogun was now available to Nobunaga. The citizens of Kyoto regarded Nobunaga as just another powerful warlord, but the disciplined behaviour of his troops, and the fact that he was the power behind the shogun, meant that he gradually gained the support of a number of the officers of the court, a trend he encouraged by arranging the restitution of some of their property.

As well as controlling the shogun, Nobunaga could rely on imperial patronage to some extent. In 1567, Emperor Ogimachi sent him a secret message congratulating him on his military skills, a ploy to enlist Nobunaga's aid in recovering some imperial property stolen by some of his enemies. Nobunaga clearly felt that fate had marked him out to govern Japan. His personal seal was engraved with the motto 'tenka-fubu' ('to bring the whole country under one sword'), and that is what he set out to do.

The new shogun, Yoshiaki, tried to impose his will on Nobunaga, a pointless exercise since Nobunaga controlled the troops who were the real power in the land. In 1570 Nobunaga gave the shogun a list of five articles, which reduced his office to a purely ceremonial role.

Nevertheless, Nobunaga provided Yoshiaki with a magnificent setting in which to play his part; he spent a vast amount of money building him a new palace, and at the same time he ordered that the imperial palace be rebuilt.

Sadly for Yoshiaki, he could not restrain himself from becoming involved in politics. Eventually he angered Nobunaga so much that, in 1573, he was deposed; he retained his title but did not wield any power, and he spent the rest of his life trying to gain supporters. His death, in 1597, marked the formal end of the Ashikaga shogunate.

Above: Toyotomi Hideyoshi earned great glory at the Siege of Inabayama, in 1566, when he led a desperate attack on the 'watergate'.

Calling the Daimyo

Early in 1570, Nobunaga asked a number of powerful daimyo to come to Kyoto, ostensibly to discuss the state of the nation and offer advice to the emperor and the shogun. However, his true motive was to see how many of them would obey what, in fact, was an order from Nobunaga himself.

One daimyo who ignored Nobunaga's request was Asakura Yoshikage of Echizen, and Nobunaga decided that he should be punished for his insolence. Assembling an army of 30,000 men, Nobunaga left Kyoto in May 1570. He needed safe passage through Omi, which should not have been a problem as his brother-in-law, Asai Nagamasa, held the area of northern Omi, and so Nobunaga's rear should have been secure.

However, Asakura Yoshikage managed to arrange an alliance between himself and Asai Nagamasa, which threatened to cut Nobunaga off from Kyoto and his base at Gifu. Nobunaga was forced to split his army into smaller units and retreat to Kyoto, thus taking the pressure off the Asakura's main stronghold of Ichi-ga-tani, which Nobunaga was preparing to attack.

A river battle

By July, Nobunaga had reformed his army and received reinforcements of 5000 men from Tokugawa Ieyasu. His first target was Odani Castle, Asai Nagamasa's stronghold. Naturally, Nagamasa asked Asakura Yoshikage for help and the two armies met on the banks of a river, the Anegawa. The River Anegawa was shallow and sluggish at that time of the year and so the two armies advanced into the middle of the river and the battle began.

Although most of the fighting was performed by units of warriors, there were individual actions by samurai reminiscent of the Gempei War. One of Nobunaga's samurai, Sasai Masayasu, armed himself with a spear and battled his way into Asakura Yoshikage's headquarters; he was only stopped when he was mown down by a volley of gunfire.

The Asakura army were put in danger by a flank attack by Honda Tadakatsu, one of Tokugawa Ieyasu's generals. To cover their retreat, an Asakura samurai, Makara Jurozaemon Naotaka, drew his no-dachi, a sword fitted with a blade over 1.5 m (5 ft) long, and challenged any of the Tokugawa samurai to fight him. He killed one Tokugawa retainer, Ogasawara Nagatada, and was then joined by his son, who was also armed with a no-dachi.

Together they repulsed many attacks by the Tokugawa warriors until they were faced by four Tokugawa samurai, who managed to drag the elder Makara from his horse and decapitate him. His son died fighting another of Nobunaga's samurai, Aoki Jozaemon. Their deaths allowed the Asakura forces to withdraw to safety, but the battle was won by Nobunaga's troops. Nobunaga expressed his gratitude to Tokugawa Ieyasu, whose attack on Asai Nagamasa's right flank had assured the final victory, with the presentation of a sword and an arrowhead, said to have belonged to Minamoto Tametomo.

Below: The site of the Battle of the Anegawa, one of Oda Nobunaga's greatest victories.

The final siege

The Asai and Asakura met their end in 1573, when Nobunaga returned to lay siege to Odani Castle. Asai Nagamasa sent his wife and three daughters to the safekeeping of her brother, Oda Nobunaga, and committed seppuku as his castle burned around him. Nobunaga had the heads of Asai Nagamasa and Asakura Yoshikage taken to Kyoto and exposed to the public gaze. Contemporary writers claimed that Nobunaga later had the heads preserved by lacquering and gilding, in order to display them at a banquet.

Nobunaga knew that of the many enemies who could prevent him realising his ambitions, the powerful army of the Ikko-ikki were among the most dangerous. He could not allow any strong alliances to form among his potential opponents, and when the Honganji sent forces into Kyoto in November 1570, to help the Miyoshi family in their struggle against Nobunaga, he decided that it was time to deal with the Ikko-ikki.

As his army became embroiled in the fight with the Ikko-ikki, the remnants of the Asai and Asakura forces defeated at the Battle of Anegawa decided that this would be a good time to attack Nobunaga through Omi province. Nobunaga withdrew from his struggle with the Ikko-ikki and turned on the Asai and Asakura, but just as he was

Left: 13th in command, General Tambe Narutada sits, fully armed, on his camp stool, holding his uchiwa (fan-shaped baton of command) in his hand.

preparing to destroy his enemies, Nobunaga's army was attacked by the warrior monks of Mount Hiei.

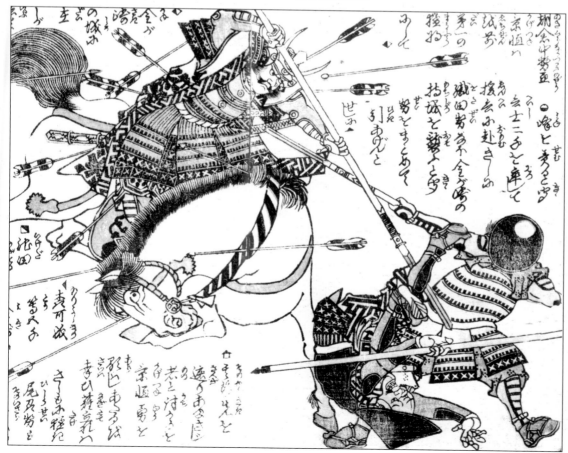

Left: Asakura Yoshikage, whose army was defeated by Oda Nobunaga at the Battle of the Anegawa.

Right: A typical sohei wearing a headcowl over his armour and wielding the monk's traditional weapon, the naginata.

Below: Noh-theatre mask of a young Buddhist monk.

Fighting the Sohei

Infuriated by the monks' intervention, Nobunaga determined to smash the power of the monks of Enryaku-ji and remove the threat they posed to himself and the capital, once and for all. He assembled an army of 30,000 men and marched on Mount Hiei.

Although the warrior monks had always been a threat to the security of Kyoto, they were still held in high esteem by many. Sakuma Nobomori and Takei Sekian, two of Nobunaga's followers, tried to persuade Nobunaga to change his mind, pointing out that for 800 years the monastery and its inhabitants had been the guardians of the imperial palace.

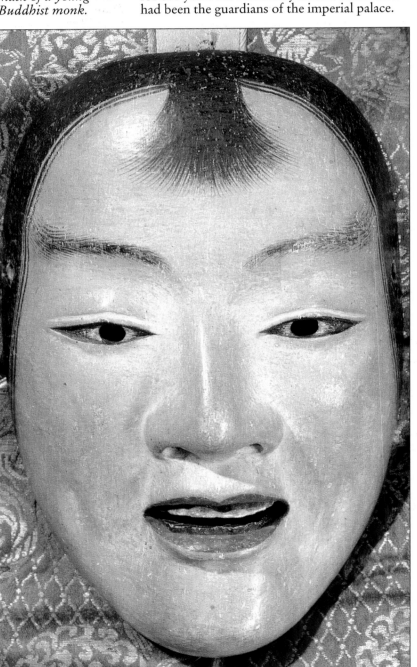

'A peril to the nation'

Nobunaga would not be swayed and answered his critics with a catalogue of the monks crimes against him. According to one of his earliest biographers, who reported his views in the 'Hoan Nobunaga-ki' ('Hoan's Life of Nobunaga'), Nobunaga declared: 'I am not the destroyer of this monastery. The destroyer of the monastery is the monastery itself....

'I have given myself to the hardships of warrior life in order that I might restrain the turbulence within the land, check the decline of imperial prestige and restore it, improve the prevailing manners and customs, and perpetuate the benefits of government and religion'.

Nobunaga described how, during his absence in the previous year, Asai and Asakura had invaded Shiga, and how, when he had returned to expel them, he had driven the rebels to the hilltop of Tsubogusa. The deep snow had retarded their flight and they were about to be slain by Nobunaga's men, when the monastic inmates of Mount Hiei came to their assistance.

He had threatened to destroy all the monastery buildings, including the central cathedral and the Shrine of the Mountain King, and decapitate all inmates, clergy and otherwise, unless they withdrew their support from the rebel side; but 'still they would not yield'.

'I do not speak falsehoods', Nobunaga declared. 'It is they who obstruct the maintenance of law and order in the country.

NOBUNAGA AND THE CHRISTIANS

Nobunaga's dislike of the political and military power of the Buddhist sects meant that he encouraged the Jesuit missionaries who arrived in Japan in the 16th century to preach the Christian message.

The first missionaries had arrived in Japan in 1549, under the leadership of the Jesuit priest, Francis Xavier (later canonised as Saint Francis Xavier). Nobunaga admired the intelligence and courage of the Jesuits and saw them as a potential check to the power of the Buddhist sects. One of the Jesuits, Luis Frois, managed to obtain a licence to preach from Shogun Yoshiaki and, under Nobunaga's protection, began to make converts among the Japanese.

Inevitably, the Jesuit missionaries aroused great hostility among the Buddhist monks. Their hostility was well-founded; where the Jesuits were able to secure the patronage of the daimyo, they ruthlessly overturned the native religious institutions, destroying ancient Shinto shrines and even forcibly converting the daimyo's people.

The Buddhist monks warned that the Jesuits were merely the advance troops of a full-scale Western invasion, but to no avail. Nobunaga's tolerance was in part dictated by his desire to keep friendly relations with the West. In 1582, four young samurai were sent on a diplomatic mission to Europe, where they met Philip II of Spain and kissed the Pope's foot. By the time of Nobunaga's death in the same year, it is estimated that there were over 150,000 Christians in Japan, and about 200 churches.

The Jesuits shrewdly concentrated their efforts on converting the ruling class, and a number of samurai were converted to the Christian faith. Takayama Ukon, the daimyo of Settsu, was baptised at the age of 10, along with his father and mother, by the Jesuit Gaspard Vilela, after his father lost a debate with the priest. In Takayama Ukon's domain it is estimated that one third of the population, about 8000 people, were baptised. It is not unusual to find samurai weapons and pieces of armour marked with Christian symbols.

Below left: Saint Francis Xavier, who took Christianity to Japan in 1549.

Below: A section from a painted screen depicting two Jesuit missionaries going about their duties among the Japanese converts.

Those who would help rebels are themselves traitors to the country. If they are not destroyed now, they will again become a peril to the nation. Therefore, not a single life should be spared'.

One of Nobunaga's retainers, Ikeda Katsusaburo, suggested that Mount Hiei should be ringed by troops at night and, as the cock crowed on the following day, the troops should move up the mountain killing everyone they met. Nobunaga accepted the plan, and on the morning of September 29, 1571, the attack began.

The monks resisted fiercely, but to no avail, By the end of the day all the monastic buildings of the ancient religious site had been put to the torch by Nobunaga's warriors and the inhabitants brutally slaughtered.

ZEN AND THE WARRIORS

Below: Daruma (in sanskrit, Bodhidharma), introduced the Zen sect into China. He is often depicted in Japanese Zen art sitting in a position of meditation. His long periods of meditation, of which the longest was nine years, led to the loss of use of his legs, and he is also said to have cut off his eyelids so that he would not lose concentration. In Japan today, 'Daruma dolls' are still bought for good luck.

A samurai could not fail in combat; the only alternative to victory was death. Given such odds, warriors searched for ways to improve their chances of winning. Highly structured methods of fighting were developed and taught, which made use of the strengths and weaknesses of a wide range of weapons, both natural and man-made.

The mental composure of a warrior when facing death was seen to be of vital importance, and anything that could strengthen a man's mind and spirit was investigated. The teachings of the Zen school were highly thought of, because Zen stresses direct experience rather than academic study, and many of the Zen masters displayed qualities of self-reliance and courage, which appealed to the samurai.

A school of Zen evolved in Kamakura, the headquarters of the Bakufu, or military government. As it was unlikely that the samurai would be familiar with the Buddhist sutras or the traditions and background of Chinese Buddhism, the method of 'shikin Zen' (on-the-instant Zen) was developed. This used koans (paradoxical statements intended to shock the mind out of its normal rut) that were derived from the everyday lives of the samurai.

While the samurai were attracted to Zen as a way of improving their fighting ability, there is no doubt that some samurai developed a profound understanding of Buddhism and achieved satori. When Hojo Tokimune died in 1284, at the age of 33, his teacher Bukko commented on his enlightenment, saying that he had thrown off earthly desires and become a spiritually advanced soul, or Bodhisattva.

Zen profoundly influenced the technical evolution of swordsmanship under the Tokugawa shogunate. The third Tokugawa shogun, Iemitsu (1604-57), was a student of the swordmaster Yagyu Tajima no kami Munenori (1571-1646). In his work 'Heihokadensho' ('Family Methods of Strategy'), Munenori showed the influence of the Zen master Takuan Soho, who helped him to clarify the importance of the swordsman's state of mind in combat. Once technique has been learned, the swordsman must develop the state of mu-shin (no mind), in which the swordsman leaves behind all feelings of fear or pride and, empty of thought, his sword is wielded in a spontaneous, natural way.

Munenori wrote: 'There is a Zen saying: "the great action is direct and knows no rules".... For everything there are instructions, there are ways and means which are usual. But the man who has attained gives them up altogether. He acts freely and spontaneously. He who is free, outside the rules, is called a man of great awareness and great action'. Takuan wrote a series of letters to Yagyu Munenori, explaining Zen in terms of swordsmanship. In the 'Fudochishinmyoroku' ('The Mysterious Record of Immovable Wisdom'), he points out that if the mind is fixed or stopped on an action then it is impossible for the swordsman to gain victory.

The trials of Matajuro

One member of the Yagyu family who had direct experience of a Zen-inspired form of training was Yagyu Matajuro. As a child, Matajuro was a promising swordsman, but because he was lazy he failed to make progress and so his family disowned him.

Determined to make something of himself, he sought out a noted swordsman named Banzo, who lived near the Kumano Machi Shrine, a

place famous for holy men who trained themselves by undergoing severe austerities. Matajuro begged Banzo to teach him the art of swordsmanship and, eventually, Banzo reluctantly agreed to accept him as a pupil and told the boy to move his possessions into his hut.

Matajuro spent his days washing, cooking and collecting firewood, but Banzo failed to teach him any techniques of swordsmanship. After three years of working as a servant, he confronted Banzo and reminded him of his promise, but the master said nothing and walked away. In despair, Matajuro decided to leave. That night, as he lay asleep, Banzo crept into his room and struck him with a wooden sword.

From that point on, Matajuro's life was nothing but pain. Without warning, Banzo would attack him, striking him painfully if he was too slow to avoid the blow. In time, however, Matajuro developed lightning-fast reactions and almost supernatural awareness, until Banzo was unable to land a blow, even when Matajuro was busy cooking rice. Without a single formal lesson, Matajuro had mastered his art, and when he returned home he took a fine sword and a certificate of mastery presented to him by Banzo.

The spiritual goal

The relationship between Zen and the martial arts was explored and explained during the Tokugawa shogunate. The various schools of swordsmanship, archery, spear fighting and other martial arts became suffused with the spirit of Zen and were taught as ways to achieve a Zen state of mind.

One of the first Westerners to experience any form of Zen training was Eugen Herrigel, who studied kyudo (archery) under the great master, Awa (1880-1939), from 1932 to 1937. In his work 'Zen in the Art of Archery', Herrigel explained that: 'By archery in the traditional sense ... the Japanese does not understand a sport, but... an ability whose origin is to be sought in spiritual exercises and whose aim consists of hitting a spiritual goal'. The association of Zen and the martial arts is by no means a thing of the past. The Zen master, Taisen Deshimaru, often held classes with highly graded martial arts masters to show the relationship between both disciplines. In Hawaii, the Zen temple of Chozen-ji still uses kyudo and other martial arts as for transmitting the Zen way, so preserving and expanding a tradition established by the samurai centuries ago.

Above: The entrance to the Ginkakuji, or Silver Pavillion, built by Ashikaga Yoshimasa, and one of the finest examples of Zen-inspired architecture and garden design in Japan.

Nobunaga's Heirs

Although Nobunaga had several sons and a number of leading retainers, who could all reasonably claim to inherit Nobunaga's position, it was decided that his infant grandson, Samboshi, should be his heir. The child was a symbol, chosen in an attempt to prevent Nobunaga's gains from being lost through fighting between his followers; in reality, it was Toyotomi Hideyoshi who held the reins of power.

Hideyoshi avenged Nobunaga's death on June 30, when he destroyed Akechi's forces at Yamazaki, south west of Kyoto. Akechi suffered a fitting end for one who had betrayed his lord; he was beaten to death by peasants as he tried to escape.

Although his relations with some of Nobunaga's powerful older retainers were sometimes a little strained, Hideyoshi rapidly consolidated his authority and began to plan for the future. Two months after the selection of Samboshi as Nobunaga's heir, Hideyoshi wrote a letter to his mistress, in which he said: 'I am [now] in Sakamoto. I will have the investitures in Omi reviewed and its castles destroyed. When there is time, I shall recover Osaka and shall station my men there. I shall order them to level the castles of the whole land to prevent further rebellions and to preserve the nation in peace for 50 years'.

The heirs divided

Hideyoshi behaved as though he were the ruler and he soon faced armed opposition from his former comrades. One of Nobunaga's former generals, Shibata Katsuie, raised troops to support the claims of Nobunaga's son, Nobutaka, in direct opposition to Hideyoshi.

Hideyoshi initially suffered a reverse when his troops were defeated in Omi, but by hard riding, Hideyoshi managed to lead a force of fresh cavalry in a surprise attack against Katsuie's army at the Battle of Shizugatake. His army scattered, Katsuie retired to the ninth floor of his castle in Kitanosho, where he first killed his wife and children and then killed himself in the traditional manner, together with more than 80 of his retainers.

A number of Hideyoshi's warriors distinguished themselves in the fighting, including Kato Kiyomasa, the son of the blacksmith from Hideyoshi's own village, and a

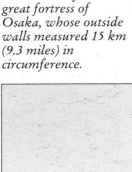

Below: Hideyoshi's great fortress of Osaka, whose outside walls measured 15 km (9.3 miles) in circumference.

man who would soon rise to become one of Hideyoshi's best generals. With Katsuie dead, Nobutaka lost all hope of gaining power. He was attacked by his brother, Nobukutsu, who was allied to Hideyoshi, and when it was obvious that any struggle was pointless, Nobutaka committed seppuku.

The next challenge to Hideyoshi came from Tokugawa Ieyasu. In 1584, their forces confronted one another on a number of occasions, fighting two major battles at Komaki and Nagakute, but by the end of 1584, peace once again existed between them.

Hideyoshi maintained the peace and increased his power by a deftly worked policy of transforming former enemies into allies. He confirmed defeated enemies in their landholdings, so allowing them to identify their interests with the survival of Hideyoshi's authority. Thus, when they took an oath of loyalty to Hideyoshi, they felt they were strengthening their own positions instead of being forced to submit. This combination of military power and subtle diplomacy meant that, by the end of 1584, Hideyoshi was in full control of Nobunaga's former possessions and was in a position to expand his territories.

The Great Hideyoshi

In 1582, Hideyoshi built Osaka Castle. The castle was to be his centre of power and he had it constructed on the site of the Ishiyama Hongan-ji, the stronghold of the Ikko-ikki. Within six years, the building had been completed.

The author of 'Tensho-ki', a laudatory biography of Hideyoshi, compared Hideyoshi to the great heroes of the past: 'There were three talents [essential] to Minamoto no Yoritomo's pacification of Japan. Yoshitsune excelled in battle skill; Kajiwara Kagetoki concentrated on worldly affairs; Hojo Tokimasa pursued the way of government.... But now Hideyoshi, with a single heart, advanced his plans, laid in provisions, and then fought his wars. Truly he is a great leader, unknown to previous ages'.

Above: A modern print depicting Hideyoshi's rapid attack on the army besieging his mountain fortress of Shizugatake.

The Southern Island

Having established himself as the heir to Nobunaga's achievements, Hideyoshi began the conquest of the remainder of Japan. He quickly defeated the daimyo in Shikkoku, allowing Chosokabe Motochika to retain control of Tosa province, while allocating large areas of land to his generals. In 1587, Hideyoshi felt ready to invade the southern island of Kyushu.

During the Sengoku Jidai, the Shimizu family from Satsuma had become the dominant force on the island. Operating from their base in Kagoshima, they established a powerful domain, which in many ways was independent of any control from Kyoto. Through trade with their near neighbours, Korea and China, the Shimizu enjoyed a thriving economy and great financial strength.

By 1585, the Shimizu clan had gained control of most of Kyushu. As they prepared to attack one of the few remaining independent daimyo, Otomo Yoshimune, he turned to Toyotomi Hideyoshi for assistance.

This was all the excuse Hideyoshi needed. In the subsequent fighting, the Shimizu forces were at first victorious, occupying the fortress of Toshimitsu and entering the capital of Bungo province, Funai, on January 24, 1587. Hideyoshi sent a force of 90,000 troops to deal

with the Shimizu clan, under the command of his half brother, Hidenaga. Remembering the lessons of the Battle of Nagashino, Hidenaga used massed gunfire to weaken the Shimizu samurai, who were forced to withdraw. Hideyoshi continued to send men and material to fight the Shimizu clan, until he controlled over 250,000 men. He gained allies from some of the Kyushu clans and began to advance on the Shimizu forces.

The opposing armies met at the River Sendai on June 6, 1587, where the overwhelming numbers of Hideyoshi's forces gained a victory. The battle was fought by huge numbers of troops in disciplined formations, but there were still moments that recalled the glories of the past. A Shimizu retainer, Niiro Tadamoto, led a wild charge of 5000 men against Hideyoshi's 170,000. The charge failed but in the fighting Niiro Tadamoto and Kato Kiyomasa fought in man-to-man combat. Although Niiro was flung from his horse, Kato Kiyomasa spared him.

Eventually, the Shimizu clan admitted defeat and put down their swords. In the settlement that followed, Hideyoshi left Satsuma in their hands but took the head of the Yoshihisa family as a hostage. Lands were also given to some of Hideyoshi's followers, including Kato Kiyomasa, so that the activities of the Shimizu could be watched.

Right: The famous daimyo from the north of Japan, Date Masamune, wears a sashimono (banner) bearing the rising sun, and has a crescent moon for his helmet crest.

HIDEYOSHI'S SWORD HUNT

As Hideyoshi established control over the territories of the daimyo, he also wanted to regulate Japanese society. To minimise the chance that anyone might rise in rebellion against his rule, Hideyoshi wanted to disarm the peasants and on August 29, 1588, he ordered that all peasant-weapons should be surrendered.

Hideyoshi maintained that he wanted the weapons gathered together so they could be melted down to make nails and spikes, which would be used in the construction of a huge statue of the Buddha. This pious work would serve a number of purposes; as well as helping the people to gain merit in this life and the next, it would impede peasant uprisings against the government.

One important social effect was the clear distinction that would now have to be made between the samurai, who were allowed to carry weapons, and the peasants, who were not. The beginnings of the rigid social structures that developed under the Tokugawa shoguns can be traced to this policy, and to the census Hideyoshi ordered to be carried out in 1590. This classified people according to their occupation, and made it difficult, if not impossible, to move from one class to another.

Left: Toyotomi Hideyoshi was probably the finest strategist of his day and his military skills enabled him to rise from humble origins to the highest position in Japan. Ironically, his own regime greatly restricted social mobility. This illustration is a hanging portrait scroll in the Hosei Niko Memorial Museum in Nakamura, Hideyoshi's birthplace.

Foreign ambitions

By 1590, Hideyoshi had accomplished the unification of Japan. The resistance of his last opponents, the Hojo of northern Honshu, ended when their castle at Odawara fell after a four month siege, and the last independent daimyo, Date Masamune, submitted to Hideyoshi at about the same time as the Hojo were defeated.

For most men, this would have been sufficient achievement for one lifetime; but Hideyoshi had other plans. In 1586, he told Mori Terumoto that he intended to conquer China, and in a letter written to his wife after the conquest of Kyushu he stated: 'By fast ships I have dispatched [orders] to Korea to serve the throne of Japan. Should [Korea] fail to serve [our throne], I have dispatched [the message] by fast ships that I will punish [that country] next year. Even China will enter my grip; I will command it during my lifetime'.

The order to invade Korea was given on April 24, 1592. Hideyoshi called upon the samurai of 32 daimyo, which gave him a force of 158,700 troops, divided into nine groups, with a reserve force of 100,000 men and a navy manned by 9200 sailors. A base was constructed in Nagoya by Kato Kiyomasa,

from which the attack on the Asian mainland could be launched.

Although Korea was the initial target, Hideyoshi described the operation as 'kara iri' ('entry into China').

Left: The warfan of Toyotomi Hideyoshi, decorated with pearls on a red silk background.

The Invasion of Korea

The first phase of Hideyoshi's invasion took about a year. Forces under the command of Konishi Yukinaga took Pusan and then rapidly made their way, virtually unopposed, to the capital of Seoul, which they occupied on June 12, 1592. The capital had been abandoned by the king and deserted by the inhabitants, and as far as the Japanese were concerned the path to China lay wide open.

However, while the Korean soldiers may have put up only a token resistance, the invading Japanese soon found that the Korean navy could and would fight. On June 16,

Below: During the Korean War a Japanese samurai, eager to capture a Chinese general, grappled with him on the edge of the sea. The unarmed combat continued underwater.

Admiral Yi Sun-shin, in command of a fleet of 'turtle ships' (an early kind of armoured gunship), attacked Japanese ships transporting troops near the island of Okpo, destroying or damaging between 40 to 60 ships.

The Japanese began to try to win the hearts and minds of the Korean people, but as the Korean troops recovered from the initial shock of the invasion, they began to fight back, aided by the spirited guerrilla activities of bands of peasants, determined to protect their land and crops. Gradually the Japanese were forced onto the defensive until, at long last, the Korean king's appeals to the Chinese court for assistance were answered.

China intervenes

A Chinese army was sent to drive the Japanese out of the old capital of Pyongyang, but the Chinese were slaughtered by Japanese troops under Konishi's command. The Chinese government finally realised the seriousness of the threat facing them and began to prepare a powerful force to deal with the Japanese. Deaths from fighting and disease began to weaken the samurai's fighting spirit; by the beginning of 1593, one third of the Japanese forces were dead or injured.

The entry of large and fresh Chinese armies, coupled with the increasing efficiency of the Korean regular and irregular forces, greatly increased the pressure on the Japanese. They were forced onto the retreat, and although they severely mauled a Chinese army which tried to retake Seoul, it was obvious that, while the Japanese could win the battles, they could not win the war.

The peace negotiations between Hideyoshi and the Chinese dragged on for over three years. Many of the Japanese troops were recalled during this this period, but Hideyoshi left a powerful rear-guard in Pusan. By December 1596, it seemed that some form of peace settlement was possible, but when Hideyoshi was informed of the Chinese proposals, which offered to make him 'King of Japan' but implicitly reduced his status to that of a vassal of the Chinese court, the peace negotiations came to an abrupt end.

Hideyoshi was so angry that he called for another invasion of Korea and China. Including the troops already in Korea, 150,000 samurai were mobilised for the new invasion. At first the Japanese were successful, but they were soon stricken by problems with supplies. Their fighting spirit was not diminished, however; during a battle fought at Sochon on October 30, 1598, Satsuma samurai commanded by Shimazu Yoshihiro, killed about 40,000 Chinese and Korean troops. Their ears were preserved in barrels of brine and sent to Kyoto, where they were buried in a mound, the Mimizuka (Ear Tomb), as a trophy.

Left: Kato Kiyomasa is shown here fighting a tiger in the mountains of Korea. Note his distinctive helmet design.

'As the dew I vanish'

On September 18, 1598, Toyotomi Hideyoshi died. He left a poem expressing his awareness of the impermanence of his life and achievements:

> 'Ah! as the dew I fall
> As the dew I vanish.
> Even Osaka fortress
> Is a dream within a dream'.

With his death, the war in Korea was effectively ended and the Japanese began to withdraw. In the final skirmishes, Admiral Yi was killed by a bullet as the last of his enemies left his homeland.

Hideyoshi had been given the title of kampaku (regent) by the court in 1585. His humble background had prevented him from being made shogun, a position that he had held in all but name. However, his most powerful ally, Tokugawa Ieyasu, did not suffer from such a lack of pedigree, and it was he who was to take command.

From Warriors to Bureaucrats

Tokugawa Ieyasu

Before he died, Toyotomi Hideyoshi tried to protect the future of his five-year-old son, Hideyori, by appointing a board of five regents, sworn to protect the child until he was old enough to inherit the position of regent. The written oath was signed on August 15, 1598, with Tokugawa Ieyasu, the most powerful of Hideyoshi's allies, singled out as Hideyori's guardian.

Tokugawa Ieyasu was born in 1541, the eldest son of a minor daimyo named Matsudaira. His father's land lay between two powerful neighbours, the Imagawa of Suruga and the Oda clan of Owari. As a young child, Ieyasu was caught up in the power struggles of the Sengoku Jidai when he was held first by Oda Nobunaga's father, Nobuhide, and then by the Imagawa clan, who held him hostage at their capital, Sumpu.

By allying himself with Oda Nobunaga and Toyotomi Hideyoshi, Ieyasu became immensely powerful; if we examine the income of the five regents we can see that Ieyasu had a revenue of 2,500,000 koku, while the next most powerful daimyo, Mori Terumoto, had less than half of this, with 1,200,000 koku (a koku is defined as the amount of rice needed to feed one man for one year).

Below: Woodcut portrait of Tokugawa Ieyasu, who founded a regime that was to last for over 200 years.

THE BATTLE FOR THE ROADS

It was clear to both commanders that control of the two main roads, known as the Tokaido and the Nakasendo, would be vital if they were to seize power. Whoever gained control of the fortresses of Gifu and Kiyosu would dominate the roads, and so, while Ishida's forces were attacking the Tokugawa stronghold of Fushimi Castle, Ieyasu sent troops to capture the two essential strongholds.

Ishida withdrew his troops to a small village named Sekigahara, about 19 km (12 miles) from his base at Ogaki. By the morning of October 20, 1600, the Western Army was in position around Sekigahara. Ieyasu began to move his forces under the cover of a heavy fog that prevented the armies from seeing one another, and unplanned skirmishes took place as various contingents of troops blundered into one another. As the fog lifted and the various bodies of samurai became visible, the fighting became more general until the armies were locked in combat.

The Western Army appeared to gain a slight advantage, but one of Ishida's apparent allies, Kobayakawa Hideaki, had already been persuaded to change sides and, at a crucial stage of the fighting, he directed his troops to attack the Western Army. Ishida Mitsunari escaped from the battle but was later captured, along with Konishi Yukinaga and Ankokuji Ekei. Konishi Yukinaga was a devout Christian and as a consequence he refused to commit seppuku. After being paraded around Osaka and Kyoto, they were taken to the execution grounds and beheaded.

Left: The site of the Battle of Sekigahara from the command post of Ishida Mitsunari, whose mon appears on the banner in the foreground.

There is a famous story that illustrates the characters of Nobunaga, Hideyoshi and Ieyasu. Comparing the fragmented state of Japan to a voiceless singing bird, Nobunaga would have said 'I'll make it sing'; Hideyoshi would threaten 'I'll kill it if it doesn't sing'; Ieyasu would smile and say 'I'll wait until it does sing'. This ability to wait for precisely the right moment was the key to Tokugawa Ieyasu's acquisition of power.

Preparing for war

There is no doubt that Hideyoshi trusted Ieyasu completely; it is said that Hideyoshi and Ieyasu once rode out together, without attendants, onto the Kanto plain. Silently, Hideyoshi took off his sword and scabbard, leaving himself defenceless, and handed them to Tokugawa Ieyasu. Pointing to Edo Bay, he said, 'make your capital there'. However, asking Ieyasu to protect his son's interests would prove extremely ill-judged.

Within a short time of Hideyoshi's death, dissent began to appear among the regents, and opposition to Ieyasu began to form around Ishida Mitsunari. Some of Hideyoshi's former supporters declared for Ishida, but as he was not a warrior he lacked credibility in the eyes of many of Hideyoshi's samurai, who preferred Ieyasu. Two groups emerged, each claiming to act in Hideyori's interests, and gradually the groups moved towards armed confrontation.

Ishida twice tried to have Ieyasu assassinated and when his plots were discovered by Kato Kiyomasa and others, they decided to kill Ishida. He managed to escape to Fushimi Castle, where Ieyasu captured him and had him sent to his own stronghold in Oami province with orders to behave himself.

Ishida's allies, usually known as the Western Army, began to prepare for war. Uesugi Kagekatsu built large numbers of strongpoints in his domain in the north and, when called upon by Ieyasu to explain his action, he told Ieyasu to mind his own business. Ishida and his supporters hoped that Ieyasu would become embroiled in a struggle with Uesugi, so leaving himself vulnerable to attack by the remainder of the Western Army. Ieyasu easily avoided the obvious trap and used his own allies, Date Masamune and Mogami Yoshiakira, to contain the Uesugi forces. Both sides spent some time attacking each other's castles, while their main forces manoeuvred for position, ready for the decisive conflict.

The New Shogun

Victory at Sekigahara left Ieyasu in a very powerful position. Such opposition as existed was in no position to cause him any serious problems. Moreover, as a descendant of the Minamoto clan, Ieyasu's lineage gave him access to the rank of shogun. In 1603, he built Nijo Castle in Kyoto, which served as a splendid backdrop for his ceremonial investment by the emperor in the same year.

However, the Battle of Sekigahara had not removed the single most important obstacle to Ieyasu's ambitions: Hideyoshi's son, Toyotomi Hideyori. Hideyori could still act as a focus for enemies of the Tokugawa, and Ieyasu's rise to power had left no shortage of these.

After Sekigahara, Ieyasu rewarded those samurai who had supported him with land taken from those who had opposed him. He also retained much of the seized land for his own use, so that his income rose to a staggering 6,500,000 koku. Naturally, this aroused a great deal of ill-feeling and a desire for revenge among his enemies, who looked to Hideyori for leadership.

Ieyasu was very careful to give the impression that he was no threat to Hideyori while he consolidated his strength, moving his

capital to Edo (renamed Tokyo in the 19th century), the stronghold of his own domains in the Kanto plain. He strengthened Edo castle and built new strongholds at key points around Edo, forming a powerful defensive network.

Concerned that the office of shogun should remain under Tokugawa control after his death, in 1605 Ieyasu transferred the title to his son, Hidetada. His retirement did not involve a real transfer of power (Ieyasu continued to rule under the title of ogushu — retired shogun);

Below: Ieyasu's magnificent mausoleum, part of the huge temple complex at Nikko. After his death, Ieyasu was worshipped as To Sho Gu, the Sun God of the East.

The Siege of Osaka Castle

Apart from a few minor skirmishes, the struggle between Ieyasu and Hideyori centred on Ieyasu's siege of Osaka Castle. Ieyasu mobilised a huge army of 180,000 men and, by the end of 1614, the defensive outposts of the castle had been captured, at some cost to Ieyasu's forces.

The castle was so well provisioned and armed that Ieyasu soon realised that a siege would take too long and a direct military assault would prove too costly. He began to negotiate with the defenders, most notably with Hideyori's mother, Yodogimi, and although they did not trust Ieyasu, they agreed to terms giving a free pardon to Hideyori and all the ronin, in return for a promise that they would raise no further rebellions.

Once the defenders had left the castle, Ieyasu gave orders for the castle moats to be filled in and the defences weakened, and early in the summer of 1615, he returned with a force of almost 250,000 men. Hideyori had managed to raise a new army of over 100,000 men, and on June 2, 1615, the two armies met at the Battle of Tenno-ji, in what proved to be the last major battle between samurai armies.

After a desperate struggle, the Tokugawa forces managed to defeat Hideyori's samurai and enter Osaka Castle. Hideyori and his family took refuge in the keep, which was blasted by cannon as the remainder of the castle was destroyed by fire. Hideyori ended his own life in the traditional manner and his mother, Yodogimi, was killed by a retainer to prevent her suffering the indignity of capture. The last of the Toyotomi, Hideyori's eight-year-old son, was decapitated. The last major threat to Tokugawa rule had been removed. A year later, Tokugawa Ieyasu died, secure in the knowledge that he had survived long enough to unify Japan and pass on the mantle of government to his son Hidetada.

Left: A section from the dramatic and highly detailed painted screen depicting the closing engagements of the Siege of Osaka Castle in 1615.

the move was calculated to further frustrate Hideyori's hopes of becoming head of state.

Hideyori continued to hold the post of kampaku, but his strength declined with the deaths of such faithful supporters as Kato Kiyomasa, Asano Nagamasa and Maeda Toshinaga. By 1614 Ieyasu judged that the time was right to remove the threat Hideyori posed to the authority of Tokugawa clan. By a process of malevolent rumour and exaggerated complaints, Hideyori was manipulated into a position whereby he no longer had any choice but to prepare for a war against the Tokugawa. He appealed to all the major daimyo for aid, but none responded. The 90,000 samurai that did rally to Hideyori's cause were mainly composed of the disaffected and the dispossessed, and included large numbers of ronin (wave men) — samurai who had lost their masters and domains.

The Tokugawa Peace

After Ieyasu's death in 1616, his policies were continued by his successors. Ieyasu's son, Hidetada, held the office of shogun from 1605 to 1622, when the post was passed on to Iemitsu, who held it from 1622 until his death in 1651.

The primary objective of the Tokugawa Bakufu was to maintain the peace and stability of the feudal system, which came to full maturity under their jurisdiction. Ieyasu indicated the course of his policies in 1615, when the 'Buke Sho Hatto' ('Rules for Martial Families') was drawn up under his direction. The 13 articles stipulated that samurai should maintain their military skills (bu) and also excel in bun (civil learning), which included such artistic pursuits as literature, history, poetry and calligraphy.

We can clearly see the change represented by Ieyasu's policy when we compare the spirit of the 'Buke Sho Hatto' with 'The Precepts of Kato Kiyomasa', written before Kato's death in 1611. These were intended for samurai raised on the harsh realities of the Sengoku Jidai. Kato believed that the samurai should concentrate on learning only those things which enhanced their abilities as warriors: 'The practice of Noh dancing is absolutely forbidden. When one unsheathes his sword, he has cutting a person down in mind. Thus, as all things are born from being placed in one's heart, a samurai who practises dancing — which is outside the martial arts — should... commit seppuku.

'One should put forth effort in matters of Learning. One should read books concerning military matters, and direct his attention to the virtues of loyalty and filial piety. Reading Chinese poetry, linked verse and waka [another type of poetry] is forbidden. One will surely become womanised if he gives his heart knowledge of such elegant, delicate refinements. Having been born into the house of a warrior, one's intentions should be to grasp the long and short swords and to die'.

Below: A painted screen showing Nijo Castle in Kyoto. The keep no longer exists.

A New Age

Kato Kiyomasa's time was over and a new age was dawning. To maintain the peace, the Tokugawa Bakufu instituted a number of policies intended to tighten their control over the daimyo. The title of 'daimyo' became clearly defined and instead of applying to any large landowner, it was restricted to describing the senior level of the samurai class; to qualify for the title, a landowner had to have a minimum income of 10,000 koku.

The class divisions in Japanese society became more rigid generally and the right to own and wear swords became exclusive to members of the samurai. Indeed, if a peasant was considered to be lacking in respect, the samurai had the right of 'kirisutogomen', which entitled him to slice off the head of the offending commoner.

The Tokugawa placed their fudai (hereditary vassals) in strategic positions around those daimyo, known as tozama (outside lords), who had submitted after the Battle of Sekigahara. Any daimyo thinking of rebelling would be open to attack from Tokugawa loyalists on their flanks and so would think twice before embarking on any warlike preparations.

All daimyo were also obliged to spend several months each year at the shogun's court in Edo, leaving their wives and children behind as hostages when they returned to their domains. This policy, known as sankin kotai (alternate attendance), meant that the daimyo had to spend large amounts of money and time travelling to and from Edo with all their attendants, thereby reducing their capability as potential rebels.

Movement around the country was strictly controlled, with barriers erected on the main routes at which travellers would be stopped to have their travel permits scrutinised. The Tokugawa officials were told to look in particular for 'de-onna iri-teppo' ('outward women and inward guns'); if a daimyo began to move his wives and family out of the Tokugawa lands, and smuggle his guns into them, it would indicate that he was preparing for war.

The Tokugawa proved to be very efficient, and the land settled down to enjoy a long spell of peace. Of course for the samurai, this posed something of a dilemma; the function of a warrior is to fight and without the stimulus of war what were they supposed to do? Certainly, their actual fighting ability suffered as their skills lost the test of continuous battlefield experience.

In 1694, the Tokugawa had to pass a law to make their samurai practise the martial arts, as it was discovered that many of the members of the Tokugawa élite unit, the O-ban (or Great Guard), could not swim or use a sword.

Inflation meant that those samurai who were on a fixed income suffered and were unable to meet the heavy obligations required of them by the Bakufu. Financial difficulties forced many samurai to borrow money from the despised merchant class, which flourished in the peaceful state of Tokugawa Japan.

Below: The progress of the daimyo along the roads of Japan was one of great splendour, governed by elaborate rules designed to bankrupt them.

Below left: Yamaga Soko was the foremost military thinker of his day. His most famous pupil was Oishi Kuranosuke, leader of the infamous 47 Ronin.

Below right: Samurai are shown here making the appropriate obeisance before the shogun, who sits behind an impenetrable screen.

Battles Overseas

As the Tokugawa Bakufu consolidated its grip on all aspects of Japanese life, small scale foreign adventures were allowed, to channel samurai energy away from any conflicts with the government. The Satsuma clan of Kyushu had fought against Ieyasu at Sekigahara, but they only received a token punishment: the head of the clan, Shimizu Yoshihiro, was ordered to abdicate his position to his son Tadatsune and become a Buddhist monk. As part of the settlement, Tadatsune was confirmed in his hereditary titles, one of which was the Lord of the Twelve Southern Islands, first granted in 1206.

The islands in question included the Ryukyus, whose inhabitants believed themselves to be under the patronage of China.

The Satsuma samurai decided that they should restore their direct control of the islands and, with Ieyasu's blessing, dispatched a force of 3000 samurai, under Kabayama Hisataka, to conquer the islands.

They landed on the main island of Okinawa and, on April 5, 1609, occupied Shuri Castle. Ieyasu Tokugawa allowed this expedition as it diverted the energies of the Satsuma samurai away from himself and strengthened Japan's barriers against foreign penetration.

Finding employment

The samurai were employed as administrators and bureaucrats, and, while they still trained in the martial arts, the modern skills of gunnery and the use of firearms were abandoned. Emphasis was placed on developing skill with swords and other medieval weapons, which were used as tools to build character.

The nature of the samurai and their arts were examined by writers such as Daidoji

A CHRISTIAN REBELLION

In 1624, Matsukara Shigemasa, the daimyo of Shimabara, devised a plan to conquer the Philippines. The idea was seriously considered by the shogunate, but Shigemasa's death in 1630 prevented him from leading the invasion. The shogun gave his son permission to go ahead in 1637, but the plans had to be shelved when a rebellion of Christian peasants, aided by a number of disgruntled ronin, broke out in his domain.

Known to history as the Shimabara Revolt, the peasant uprising was to have a significant impact on the policy of the Tokugawa shogunate. From their base in Hara Castle, on the Shimabara peninsula, around 37,000 peasants and ronin managed to resist the attacks of an army of over 50,000 samurai. The attackers were forced to use heavy guns, supplied by the Dutch, to batter the defenders, and it was only when starvation weakened the garrison that the castle fell.

The fact that it took so many samurai so long to dispose of mere peasants indicates a decline in the fighting spirit and skill of the samurai. The rebellion shocked the shogunate, which saw it as confirmation of the subversive influence of Christianity and determined to close off Japan from pernicious foreign influences in the future.

Policies were adopted excluding all foreigners from Japanese territory. Trade with the Portuguese was broken off and, in 1640, the Dutch were expelled from Hirado. Moreover, the Japanese were forbidden to travel outside their own country on pain of death. Some contact was maintained with the West through a Dutch trading mission at Deshima island, but foreign religion, ideas, books and technology were banned or severely controlled. Japan had been transformed into 'sankoku' — 'the closed-country'.

Left: This modern aluminium statue is of the mysterious and enigmatic leader of the Shimabara Rebellion in 1638, Amakusa Shiro.

Yuzan (1637-1730), Yamaga Soko (1622-85), and the Zen master, Takuan (1573-1645). Out of this literary reflection, a new view of the role of the samurai emerged, which stressed his function as a role model to the rest of society.

The samurai class as a whole were now expected to act as the moral and spiritual exemplars for the nation. The 18th century poet Moto Mokuami captured the flavour of his times when he wrote:

'Sweat dripping down
As you drill away at
   the arts of the sword:
That they're no use,
May this reign be praised'.

Even among fencing masters, ideas arose which would have been anathema to the samurai of the Gempei wars or the Sengoku Jidai. In 1768, Kimura Kyoho wrote 'Kenjutsu Fushiki Hen' ('The Unknown in The Art of Swordsmanship'). In his opinion: 'The perfect swordsman avoids quarrelling or fighting. Fighting means killing. How can one human being bring himself to kill a fellow being?

'We are all meant to love one another and not to kill.... We are moral beings, we are not to lower ourselves to the status of animality. What is the use of becoming a fine swordsman if he loses his human dignity? The best thing is to be a victor without fighting. The sword is an inauspicious instrument to kill in some unavoidable circumstances. When it is to be used, therefore, it ought to be the sword that gives life and not the sword that kills'.

ART AND THE SAMURAI

Below: A tea bowl filled with the green tea used only in the tea ceremony, accompanied by an ornamental cake. It is framed by the view of the tea garden in the grounds of the former mansion of the Matsuura daimyo of Hirado.

While the essence of a samurai's life lay in acquiring skills in the art of war and practising the code of Bushido, in times of peace he was also exhorted to cultivate more peaceful pursuits. As Daidoji Yuzan advised in the 'Budo Shoshinshu' (written in the 17th century): 'Though Bushido naturally implies first of all the qualities of strength and forcefulness, to have this one side only developed is to be nothing but a rustic samurai of no great account'. Yuzan went on to recommend that a samurai 'should take up verse making or Teaism... for if he does not study he will not be able to understand the reason of things either past or present'.

Over the centuries, many samurai became accomplished poets. Minamoto Sanetomo (1192-1219), the third Kamakura shogun, published an anthology of his poems, the 'Kinkaishu', and Taira Tadanori (1144-84), the younger son of Taira Kiyomori, achieved fame as a poet. Even during the constant fighting of the Sengoku Jidai, some samurai developed artistic talents to match their martial accomplishments. Date Masamune (1565-1636), the daimyo of Sendai in northern Honshu, was known as the 'One-eyed Dragon' after being wounded in battle. He had cut away the damaged eye as it hung down his cheek, to prevent an enemy seizing it during the fighting. It might be supposed that such a man would have no time for poetry, but he was so moved by the beauty of Mount Fuji that he felt inspired to write:

> 'Each time I see Fuji,
> It appears changed
> And I feel I view it
> Ever for the first time'.

'A world of recluses'

While poetry, calligraphy and other literary arts attracted samurai devotees, perhaps the most popular mode of artistic expression with the samurai class as a whole was the art of Cha no Yu, or the tea ceremony. Deriving from rituals followed in Chinese Buddhist temples, the tea ceremony was introduced to Japan by the monks Eisai (1141-1215) and Dai-O (1236-1308). The abbot of Daitokuji, Ikkyu (1398-1481), passed on the art to his disciple Shuko (1422-90), under whose patronage the tea ceremony ceased to be the exclusive province of Zen priests and attracted a secular following.

As a Zen-inspired art, Cha no Yu aims to develop a sense of natural simplicity; a direct experience of reality, uncluttered by intellectual considerations. The utensils and setting selected for the ceremony reflect this aim, being made of plain, natural materials.

The Zen master, Takuan (1573-1645), described the ideal conditions for the tea ceremony: 'Let us then construct a small room in a bamboo grove or under trees, arrange streams and rocks and plant trees and bushes.... In this room we can enjoy the streams and rocks as we do the rivers and mountains in Nature... we listen quietly to the boiling water in the kettle, which sounds like a breeze passing through the pine needles, and become oblivious of all worldly woes and worries; we then pour out a dipperful of water from the kettle, reminding us of the mountain stream, and our mental dust is wiped off. This is truly a world of recluses, saints on earth'.

Left: A tea bowl by Chojiro made in 1589 in the raku style, which involved applying raw materials as glazes prior to the actual firing, which was done rapidly and at a high temperature. All tea bowls were highly prized, often being preferred as a gift above the alternative of a fine sword.

The great warlords, Oda Nobunaga and Toyotomi Hideyoshi, were both enthusiastic patrons of the tea ceremony. Hideyoshi was so fascinated by the practice that, in 1587, he staged a vast public event open to anyone interested in the art of Cha no Yu; more than 1500 small enclosures were erected in the Kitano woods to accommodate enthusiasts from all over Japan, and on the first day of the festival Hideyoshi and his tea masters served over 800 guests.

Some of Hideyoshi's warriors regarded the tea ceremony with suspicion. Kuroda Yoshitaka observed that it was dangerous to sit so close to a possible enemy while unarmed. But even he conceded that the ceremony might have some value; the isolation and calm of the tea house provided the ideal location for private discussions of sensitive military matters. For many samurai, the tea ceremony became simply another means to display their wealth and sense of fashion, and vast sums were paid for the pottery, bamboo and metal utensils used in the ceremony.

Sen no Rikyu

Hideyoshi employed the greatest of the tea masters, Sen no Rikyu (1521-91), under whose influence the tea ceremony achieved the form still seen today. Sen no Rikyu stressed the development of a refined simplicity, known in Japanese aesthetics as 'wabi' and 'sabi', a rustic naturalness or poverty, in which good taste is expressed in a harmony of muted colours and simple shapes.

It is believed that Hideyoshi often consulted Sen no Rikyu on matters of policy, and it seems likely that this involvement in politics led to Sen no Rikyu's death, causing Hideyoshi first to send the great tea master into exile, and then order him to commit seppuku. In 1591, after performing the tea ceremony for the last time, Sen no Rikyu took his own life; it is a measure of Hideyoshi's respect for him that Sen no Rikyu, who was born into the merchant classes, was accorded the honour of ending his life like a samurai.

While the samurai pursued various aesthetic and artistic pastimes, it is important to remember that there was always a suspicion that the acquisition of literary or artistic skills might weaken a warrior's fighting ability, corrupting their élite code with the values and practices of the merchant classes. For, as Daidoji Yuzan warned: 'Rather than becoming such a dilettante, it would be better to have no knowledge of the Way of Tea at all, and to be unpolished to the point of not even knowing how to lift the bowl. These words are for the understanding of warriors'.

Left: Sen no Rikyu, the great tea master who was the confidant of Toyotomi Hideyoshi.

The 47 Ronin

One of the most important thinkers in defining the role of the samurai in Tokugawa Japan was Yamaga Soko (1622-85). Yamaga wrote a series of works, which explored and defined 'The Warrior's Creed' (Bukyo) and 'The Way of the Samurai' (Shido, or Bushido). His ideas profoundly influenced Oishi Kuranosuke, a retainer of Asano Naganori (1667-1701), the daimyo of Ako, in Harima province.

Below: The 47 Ronin gather for their dawn raid on the mansion of Kira to avenge their late master.

Lord Asano was one of a number of daimyo ordered by Shogun Tokugawa Tsuneyoshi to entertain envoys from the emperor when they visited the shogun's court at Edo. It was important that, as a representative of the shogun, Lord Asano should not offend against the complicated imperial etiquette, so Kira Yoshinaka, an acknowledged expert on etiquette, was appointed to teach Asano the correct way to receive the imperial envoys.

Kira made it obvious that he expected Asano to bestow lavish gifts in return for his instruction, whereas Asano was of the opinion that it was Kira's duty to teach him. This led to bad feeling between them, and when Kira insulted Asano in public, Asano drew his wakizashi (short sword) and cut Kira on the forehead. To draw a weapon in the shogun's palace was a serious offence and the act of wounding a shogunal official made it even worse. There was only one punishment fit for a daimyo; Asano was ordered to commit seppuku, and his fief was confiscated.

Oishi's vendetta

After Asano's death, his wife shaved her head and became a nun and his retainers lost their positions and became ronin. Oishi Kuranosuke called the ronin together and asked them to join him in killing Kira in order to revenge their lord; 46 answered his call and they began to make preparations for Kira's death.

Kira, realising that he was at risk, surrounded himself with armed guards, so Oishi decided to wait and strike when success was certain. To convince Kira that he was safe, the 47 ronin separated and disguised themselves; some became craftsmen or merchants, while Oishi left his family and associated with prostitutes and the low life of Edo, often appearing drunk in the street and brawling with passers by. On one occasion, a samurai from Satsuma saw Oishi insensible in the street and spat on him, saying he was not fit to be a samurai.

The plan worked and gradually Kira relaxed his vigilance and dismissed his guards. On December 14, 1702, the ronin gathered together and collected arms and armour they had previously hidden away. Dividing into two groups, they attacked Kira's mansion from the front and rear and, although Kira's guards put up a strong resistance, the ronin eventually caught him. In deference to his rank, Oishi invited Kira to commit seppuku, but he refused to speak, so Oishi cut off his head with the same dagger that Asano had used to commit seppuku. The head was put in a bucket and taken to Asano's tomb in Sengakuji temple, where it was laid as an offering in front of Asano's grave.

The ronin then gave themselves up to the authorities. While there was a great deal of sympathy for their actions, the Tokugawa Bakufu would not allow their loyalty to their

THE CLOSED COUNTRY

Although the story of the 47 ronin confirms the continuation of the warrior code into the 18th century, the reality of Japan under the Tokugawa regime was increasingly at odds with samurai traditions. After a century of peace, the martial qualities of many of the samurai were atrophied through disuse; atrophy which a further century of Tokugawa rule did nothing to alleviate.

The decline in standards did not pass unnoticed. In his work 'Hagakure' ('The Hidden Leaves'), written in 1716, Yamamoto Tsunetomo observed that: '...now when young samurai get together, if there is not just talk about money matters, loss and gain, secrets, clothing styles or matters of sex, there is no reason to gather together at all. Customs are going to pieces'.

The breakdown in samurai customs reflected wider social changes; changes that undermined the rigid feudal system upheld by the Tokugawa shogunate. The rise of a wealthy merchant class was accompanied by a gradual transformation of Japan's economy. Where rice had traditionally been the means of exchange and the standard of wealth in Japanese society, money became more and more important, particularly in the cities.

The samurai, whose incomes were fixed in terms of rice, were increasingly at the mercy of the merchants who could convert their rice into money. Economic development left the samurai poorer and often debt-ridden; some were even prepared to sell their samurai status, adopting the children of the new rich in exchange for money.

The Tokugawa shoguns were careful not to enable foreign powers to take advantage of Japan's internal tensions. But while their policy of restricting contact with foreign ideas worked for two and a half centuries, they could not deter external forces forever. Once again, the samurai would face an invasion of foreigners, but this time there would be no kami-kaze to save them.

Left: As the years of war passed into distant memory, the image of the samurai was reduced from that of the noble warrior to that of a character in a kabuki play, to be cheered or laughed at by theatre-goers from the despised merchant classes. This is one of the best known samurai roles, that of the title role in the play 'Shibaraku'. Note the extravagant make-up, costume and sword.

lord to disrupt the laws forbidding vendettas and the ronin were ordered to commit seppuku. Their bodies were buried in Sengakuji next to their lord, whom they had served faithfully to the death. They were joined by the body of the Satsuma samurai, who committed seppuku in front of Oishi's grave to atone for the insults he had given.

The incident provoked tremendous interest and comment, reminding the Japanese that the samurai spirit still existed among some of the warrior class. The Kabuki writer Chikamatsu wrote a play based on the event, which was an instant success. The famous 'Chushin-gura' ('A Treasury of Loyal Hearts') is still a popular favourite among theatre audiences.

In Sengakuji the graves and their associated cherry trees are still venerated as symbols of loyalty and the true samurai spirit. Even today, Japanese visit all the graves in turn, burning incense and praying for the souls of the 47 ronin of Ako.

Left: The graves of the 47 Ronin at the Sengakuji temple, in Tokyo.

The Black Ships

Changes from Outside

By the end of the 18th century, forces beyond the control of the Tokugawa Bakufu had begun to intrude on the tightly controlled system administered by the government. A rising population, coupled with civil disturbances involving peasants and ronin, caused problems internally, while the expansion of powerful nations into the Pacific brought the threat of change from the outside.

In 1792, Catherine the Great of Russia sent an envoy, Lieutenant Adam Laxman, to Hokkaido in order to negotiate a trade agreement with the Bakufu. He was followed, in 1804, by another envoy, Rezanov; in both cases the Tokugawa Bakufu showed no interest in opening Japanese ports to Russian ships.

In this same period, American expansion into the west and the growth of the American whaling industry meant that an increasing number of American ships could be found in the Pacific. It was only a matter of time before the American

Below: A posed photograph of a melancholy daimyo and his retainer, symbolic of the passing of the samurai age, and the reluctant acceptance of foreign ideas.

sailors' need for supplies and shelter from storms, and the desire of American industrialists for new markets, would lead them to Japan.

The American government sent two missions to Japan; in 1846, Commander James Biddle sailed his ship into Edo Bay, and in 1849, Commander Glynn visited Nagasaki. Neither mission achieved anything, except the rescuing of 15 shipwrecked American sailors by Commander Glynn.

'The vertex of the earth'

The escalation of Western activities near Japan prompted considerable public outcry among the Japanese. One writer, Aizawa Seishisai (1762-1863), incensed by the West's intrusion, proposed that the Western 'barbarians' should be dealt with in exactly the same manner as earlier invaders had been: they should be fought and destroyed.

In the preface to his work, 'Shinron' ('New Proposals'), written in 1825 when Western ships began to appear more frequently in Japanese waters, Aizawa stated: 'Japan's position at the vertex of the earth makes it the standard for the nations of the world....

'Today, the alien barbarians of the West, the lowly organs of the legs and feet of the world, are dashing about across the seas, trampling other countries underfoot, and daring, with their squinting eyes and limping feet, to override the noble nations.... Unless great men appear, who rally to the assistance of Heaven, the whole natural order will fall victim to the predatory barbarians, and that will be all'.

Aizawa went on to compare the arrival of Western ships with the invasions of the Mongols: 'When the Mongols were insolent, Hojo Tokimune stood resolute.... The men who were called upon to sacrifice themselves, responded by defying death in a body, as if the entire nation were of one mind. Their loyalty and patriotism were such as to bring forth a storm and hurricane that smashed the foe at sea.

'"Put a man in a position of inevitable death, and he will emerge unscathed", goes the saying. The ancients also said that the nation would be blessed if all in the land lived as if the enemy were right on the border. So I say, let a policy for peace or for war be decided upon first of all, thus putting the entire nation into the position of inevitable death. Then, and only then, can the defence problem be easily worked out'.

Commodore Perry

From 1839 until 1842, the British and the Chinese fought the Opium War. The war resulted in a humiliating defeat for the Chinese Empire and the acquisition of Hong Kong by the British. Western nations were quick to see that China was weak and had no answer to their superior military technology.

Taking this lesson to heart, the Americans once again turned their attentions to Japan. A squadron of eight ships — a quarter of the American navy — was put under the command of Commodore Matthew C. Perry. Perry's task was clear; he was to obtain care and protection for stranded American sailors, together with permission for American ships to enter Japanese ports to buy provisions, refit, and to trade.

Perry did not have to rely on persuasion alone to accomplish his task. His orders stated: 'It is manifest, from past experience, that arguments or persuasion addressed to this people, unless they be seconded by some imposing manifestations of power, will be utterly unavailing.... Therefore, direct the commander of the squadron to proceed with his whole force to such a point on the coast of Japan as he may deem most advisable, and there endeavour to open a communication with the government, and, if possible, to see the emperor in person, and deliver him the letter of introduction from the President'.

If persuasion did not work then Perry was not to use force, but should warn the Japanese that any future abuse of American sailors, either by the

Left: A portrait of Commodore Matthew Perry, accompanied, rather ironically, by a poem from Yoshida Shoin, who was one of the statesmen most fiercely opposed to the opening up of Japan.

government or inhabitants, would lead to the guilty party being 'severely chastised'.

The message was clearly understood by those Japanese who saw four of Perry's squadron arrive at Uraga, at the mouth of Edo Bay, on July 8, 1853. The appearance of the vessels, described as 'four black ships of evil mien', left no doubt that they were warships. The mysteries of steam propulsion and the obvious fire-power of the artillery on the ships, impressed the Japanese authorities, who eventually accepted the letter from President Fillmore to the emperor and duly delivered it to the shogun.

Left: Commodore Perry lands in Japan in 1854.

The Bakufu Responds

The implications of Perry's proposals sent shockwaves through the country. The Bakufu was so worried that it took the unprecedented step of seeking advice from all the daimyo and the imperial court. The Emperor Komei said that he wanted the shogun to drive the barbarians away from the sacred soil of Japan; that was, after all, the reason why he held supreme military power.

Komei's direct appeal for military action gained the monarchy support from those samurai, such as Tokugawa Nariaki, who proposed the policy of 'sonno-joi' ('revere the emperor and expel the barbarians').

Nariaki advocated a war to punish the Americans for their temerity in disturbing the tranquillity of Japan. But other voices advised caution. These moderates included Abe Masahiro, the president (roju) of the shogun's advisory council, who was aware that Japan could not drive off a nation armed with modern weapons.

The moderates managed to persuade the majority that some compromise was necessary. When Perry returned, in February 1854, the shogunate signed the Treaty of Kanagawa, which opened the ports of Shimoda and Hakodate to foreign trade and allowed for an American consul to settle in Shimoda.

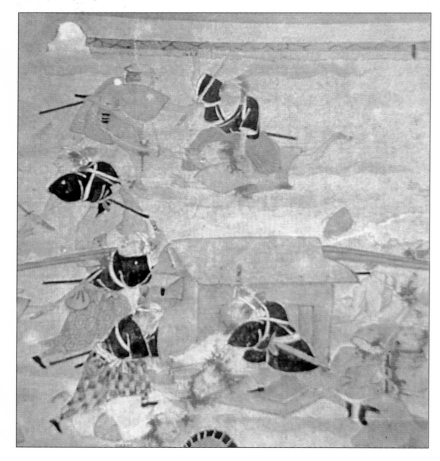

The conservatives hoped that by signing the treaty they would gain enough time to re-arm with Western weapons and then fight the barbarians on their own terms, believing that ultimately their superior fighting ability would bring them victory.

However, once the door had been opened, other nations wanted to enter. Admiral Sir James Stirling arrived in Edo Bay to sign the first treaty between Japan and Great Britain, on October 14, 1854, and similar treaties were later signed with the Russians and the Dutch.

Tokugawa Nariaki was appointed to strengthen the coastal defences, and modern warships and weapons were ordered from Dutch shipbuilders and armament manufacturers. In 1855, Dutch instructors were brought to Nagasaki to teach the samurai techniques of modern naval warfare, but they reported that the Japanese emphasis on social rank and dislike of firearms meant that their pupils made very slow progress.

According to the Treaty of Kanagawa, the Americans had the right to appoint a consul to Japan. In 1856, Townsend Harris arrived to take up his post. He was not well received; Tokugawa Nariaki's son wanted to decapitate him. But eventually, after months of negotiation, in which the threat of Western force played a significant role, Harris managed to persuade the Bakufu's representative, Ii Naosuke, that Japanese interests would be best served by a new commercial treaty with the United States that would open more ports and allow foreigners to live in Japan.

THE MEN OF HIGH-PURPOSE

The murder of Ii Naosuke was the first in a series of attacks aimed at any official thought to be pro-foreign. The attackers described themselves as shishi (men of high purpose). Their task, as far as they were concerned, was to rid Japan of the traitors who had allowed foreign barbarians to taint the sacred islands of the gods with their presence. They were also keen to cut down any foreigners who might be foolish enough to offer themselves as targets.

In January 1861, Townsend Harris lost his interpreter, Henry Heusken, when he was killed by two ronin as he rode home at night. The attacks increased in severity, and, on July 11, 1861, the British Legation in Edo was attacked by 15 shishi, who were fought off by Sir Rutherford Alcock and his staff, armed with rifles and revolvers.

The Legation was supposed to be protected by 150 Tokugawa samurai, all of whom were asleep when the shishi attacked. Although none of the British diplomats were killed, Laurence Oliphant was seriously wounded when he was forced to defend himself with a riding whip against a samurai armed with a sword. His life was saved when the samurai was shot by Morrison, another of the defenders.

It would not be long before attacks of this kind prompted the Western powers to retaliate.

Below: A print showing an attack on foreigners by xenophobic samurai at Namamugi, near Yokohama.

Grass-root Heroes

The conservatives were furious about the new treaty. Not only did it open the way for an increased foreign presence in Japan, but it also stipulated that offences committed by foreign nationals in Japan would be dealt with by consular courts rather than by the Japanese authorities.

This was regarded as an affront to Japanese sovereignty, and when the same terms were extended to Great Britain, Russia, Holland and France, the conservatives threatened violence. Some daimyo were arrested and others were executed. Although the Bakufu's policies were enforced, there was a strong feeling that the Tokugawa shogunate was betraying Japan to the foreigners.

Yoshida Shoin was one of the samurai who criticised the Tokugawa shogunate, and for that he was executed in 1859. Observing the political situation of the day, he wrote: 'The feudal lords are content to look on while the shogunate carries on in a high-handed manner. Neither the lords nor the shogun can be depended upon [to save the country], and our only hope lies in grass-root heroes'.

The 'grass-root heroes' soon appeared. On the morning of March 24, 1860, Ii Naosuke, the tairo (senior counsellor) to the shogun, was being carried in a closed kago (or palanquin) to a meeting with the shogun. As his procession approached the Sakurada-mon (Cherry-field Gate), it was attacked by armed samurai, who cut down the guards and beheaded Ii Naosuke.

Right: A samurai in an elaborate kami-shiomo (the combination of hakama trousers and winged jacket over a kimono). Note the Western clock at his side.

The West Attacks

In 1862, four Englishmen were out riding near Yokohama when the daimyo of Satsuma, Shimazu Hisamitsu, passed by with his retinue. As the foreigners did not dismount and bow to the daimyo, his samurai felt that they were not showing enough respect so they attacked, killing one of them, Charles Richardson, and wounding the other three.

The incident provoked a furious response from the British. The British government demanded a large indemnity from the shogun and the Satsuma daimyo, as well as punishment for the attackers.

In August 1863, the Royal Navy sent a force of warships to bombard the Satsuma capital, Kagoshima, an action which so impressed the Satsuma samurai with the effectiveness of the British ships and guns that they subsequently ordered modern warships from British yards and approached the Royal Navy to train the crews.

The Choshu samurai decided to challenge the naval power of the West by closing the straits of Shimonoseki to all foreign vessels. On September 5, 1864, an allied squadron of 16 British, French and Dutch warships, as well as a small steamer, the Ta-Kiang — chartered by the American Minister and flying the Stars and Stripes, forced the straits and shelled the guns

Below: An engraving from an 1864 edition of 'The Illustrated London News', showing the bombardment of Shimonoseki.

manned by Choshu samurai. On the morning of September 6, a force of 1900 sailors, Royal Marines and Royal Engineers landed to take and destroy the enemy guns.

A report published in the 'Illustrated London News' on November 19, 1864, described the action as a group of Royal Marines and Royal Engineers approached a Japanese battery: 'It was here that Captain Alexander was disabled by a severe wound in the foot, and the storming party were assailed with round shot and shell from the battery, as well as musketry and arrows from the Japanese (about 600) by whom it was defended. The position was covered by a wooden stockade, behind which some huts or barracks were erected. The enemy, however, did not wait for the approach of our men, but took to flight, making an attempt to set fire to their magazines. The flames were soon extinguished, and a large quantity of arms and ammunition fell into the hand of our men'.

Captain John Moresby of HMS Argus was awarded the Victoria Cross for his part in the action. He witnessed the attack and reported that, although outnumbered: 'Our men never checked, and rushing on, swarmed over the wall and won the stockade, the enemy disappearing into the bush'.

This single action clearly illustrates the decline of the samurai's fighting spirit and lack of technical skill. They were prepared to shoot from behind cover, but when faced with the possibility of man-to-man combat, which their training with the sword should have prepared them for, they ran away and abandoned their weapons to a numerically inferior force. Their ancestors, who had faced and defeated the Mongols, would have wept with shame.

Dealing with the invaders

One effect of this demonstration of naval power was to persuade the samurai of Satsuma and Choshu that only by reconciling their differences and joining their forces could they hope to remove the shogunate and deal with the invaders. In the Choshu domain, a group of young samurai were of the opinion that reform of the clan's army was needed before any real change in the nation could come about.

The daimyo of Choshu, Mori Takachika, gave the task of reorganising his forces to the young strategist, Takasugi Shinsaku. At an interview with his lord on June 6, 1863, Takasugi expressed his opinion that: 'The stipendiary samurai have become soft through years of peace and idleness. Their martial prowess has been dulled, and to reinvigorate an army one must recruit volunteers with spirit, courage, and skill, regardless of their class, whether they be samurai, peasant or artisan'. With his lord's permission, Takasugi organised units of kiheitai (surprise troops), which

Above: A wounded 'shishi' of the Restoration Wars.

proved their worth when the shogunate sent an army of 150,000 men to punish Choshu for an attack by its forces on Kyoto, in August 1864. Although the Choshu daimyo surrendered to the government, the leaders of the kiheitai continued the struggle and eventually seized control of the fief for themselves.

In the summer of 1866, the shogunate sent a second army to deal with the new leaders of the Choshu samurai. On this occasion, the Satsuma and other powerful domains refused to help the government and the re-organised and re-armed Choshu forces fought the Bakufu's army to a standstill. The humbled shogunate was forced to sue for peace.

The Meiji Restoration

Clearly, the Tokugawa Bakufu was in the throes of a major crisis. The deaths of Emperor Komei and Shogun Iemochi brought a new shogun, Keiki, to power in January 1867. Keiki made attempts to reform the Tokugawa administration, but he soon realised that to avoid a full scale civil war the Tokugawa Bakufu would have to come to an end.

In November 1867, he accepted the need for an imperial restoration. Some of the Tokugawa daimyo would not give up their power easily and some fighting took place between Tokugawa and imperial supporters; but in the end the imperial forces, commanded by Saigo Takamori, easily defeated the Tokugawa troops, despite being outnumbered by three to one.

The only serious resistance to the imperial forces came from Tokugawa supporters in the province of Echigo, but eventually the imperial forces gained the upper hand and the long reign of the Tokugawa Bakufu was finally brought to a close. Emperor Komei's 14-year-old son, Mutsuhito, was declared emperor.

He took the name Meiji, which means 'Enlightened Rule'. Consequently, the end of the system of military government and the resumption of power by the emperor is known as the Meiji Restoration.

The death knell

To avoid the possibility of history repeating itself and a new shogun emerging, the imperialists issued a 'Five Articles Oath' on April 8, 1868. The oath indicated some of the radical changes planned by the new regime.

The first article stipulated that: 'Deliberative assemblies shall be widely established and all matters decided by public discussion'. This was not a call to democracy but a reassurance to samurai domains as yet unrepresented in the government, that their interests would not be ignored.

The real key to the imperialists policy lay in article five, which stated: 'Knowledge shall be sought throughout the world so as to strengthen the foundations of imperial rule'. This would prove to be the death knell of the samurai. They were an integral part of a feudal system that depended upon a strict separation of classes and the concentration of military technology and power in the hands of a few. An open country, actively seeking knowledge from abroad, would be susceptible to rapid change, and change would destroy the raison d'être of the samurai.

Emperor Meiji and his advisers introduced sweeping reforms from his new capital at Edo, which was renamed Tokyo (eastern capital). The new government divided the daimyo's domains into prefectures, appointing the former owners as governors. In 1871, a new imperial army of 10,000 men was formed from Satsuma, Choshu and Tosa samurai and placed under the command of Saigo Takamori. Various government ministries were formed following western models, and then, in 1873, came the greatest change of all.

Yamagata Aritomo returned from an inspection tour of Europe with the firm conviction that Japan needed a modern army based on European models, with troops conscripted from all classes. The establishment of an army based on conscription fatally undermined the status of the warrior class.

This blow to samurai pride was compounded by a law of 1876 ending the wearing of swords. As a class, the samurai were obsolete. Their traditional profession was open to peasants and the wearing of their swords forbidden; unless they changed to suit conditions, they would have no place in the new Japan.

Below: Emperor Meiji and his wife, from a Western-style print.

THE MONEY OF TEARS

For many of the samurai the reforms of Japanese society spelled economic ruin. The constitutional consequences of the Meiji Restoration meant that about 2,000,000 samurai no longer had a domain to belong to and so had no form of income.

The government paid them a small pension, but it was never enough. To feed their families, some samurai sold off their land and possessions. When things became really desperate, several of them were forced to sell their swords, an act which would never have been contemplated before. The money raised by such sales was known as 'namida no kane' ('the money of tears'), a term that vividly illustrated the feelings of the warriors as they were forced to part with their most precious possessions in order to survive.

Some of the samurai became merchants or entered other occupations. Many found new employment as members of the police force. According to Isabella Bird, a Victorian travel-writer who visited Japan in 1878, the 23,000-strong Japanese police force was principally composed of 'gentlemanly-looking' members of the samurai class.

However, there were others who, unable to adjust to the changes, simply waited and dreamed of a more glorious past. One inspector wrote in a report: 'The shizoku (ex-samurai) [in Ishikawa] are lazy and inactive, and still have not shed their old habits. Although they have been loaned funds to establish enterprises, only a few have achieved their goals. Most of them do not work and thus produce nothing. As the days go by, they do not display the spirit to help themselves and just depend on others for their living'.

Below: An old samurai, whose life as a warrior has now ceased to have any meaning, kneels to accept his fate.

Left: The embassy of Prince Iwakura, which toured the Western nations during the early 1870s. This was the first use of the rising sun as the Japanese national flag, as distinct from merely being an individual daimyo's emblem.

FAMILY CRESTS

The Mon were the heraldic crests worn by samurai on their clothing and armour in order to identify which clan a samurai belonged to or served. In battle, the mon were useful to help identify which side a samurai was fighting on. As warfare became more organised and disciplined, it became common for warriors to fasten a sashimono (banner) to their armour that clearly displayed their mon.

Originally, mon were simple designs drawn from nature or geometric patterns, but in time political alliances or marriage caused some of the simple mon to become joined into extremely complex designs. The earliest record of the mon of the military houses was compiled in the 1460's. Known as the 'Kenmon Shoka Mon', it records 261 crests of samurai who took part in the Onin War.

By the 16th century, the practice of joining simple mon into complex designs ceased. This was partly due to the need for simplicity (mons had to be easily identifiable), but it was also because many of the domains represented by the mon ceased to exist in the chaos of the Sengoku Jidai.

As a mon was a symbol of the samurai's lord, it had to be respected. In Daidoji Yuzan's 'Budo Shoshinshu', a work intended to record the correct behaviour of a samurai, Daidoji tells us: 'There are times when a warrior who is serving in attendance may receive, by his lord's wishes, a ceremonial robe or ceremonial undergarment to which is affixed the lord's family crest. It is important to understand that when wearing the undergarment with the lord's crest, one should wear a ceremonial robe with his own crest, and when wearing the ceremonial robe with the lord's crest, he should wear the ceremonial undergarment with his own crest.

'On the other hand, were he to wear both garments with the lord's crest, he would appear to be on the same level as the close relatives of the lord, and this would be extremely discourteous... Moreover, when the ceremonial undergarment one has received becomes old and is no longer wearable, one should cut off the lord's family crest and burn the garment.

'The reason is that in the case of warriors of low rank, their wives and servants are ordered to wash old undergarments; and being women, they will, without any thought at all, make an old garment... into a cloth lining for the waist down, and from that, unknowingly, into bedclothes or underwear.

'Thus desecrating the lord's family crest, one will lose divine favour and, unawares, incur the master's punishment'.

The tea master's duel

The responsibilities incurred by wearing a mon are illustrated in a famous tale, often called 'The Tea Master and the Ronin'.

Towards the end of the 17th century, the daimyo of Tosa visited Edo to see the shogun. In his retinue he included his tea master, who, like the other retainers, wore the lord's mon on his clothing. Although he was not a warrior, the tea master wore the two swords of the samurai class.

One day, while out sight-seeing, the tea master was accosted by a ronin, who challenged him to fight. The ronin realised that he was not really a swordsman and thought that he might be able to frighten him into parting with some money in order to save his life. However, the tea master replied that,

Below: A group of samurai wearing kami-shimo, showing various designs of mon.

although he was not a swordsman, he would fight the ronin to prevent his lord losing face, but the ronin must give him a couple of hours to prepare. The ronin agreed and a time was set for the duel.

The tea master had noticed a martial arts dojo nearby and he went to the senior master of the dojo and asked for instruction in how to die like a true samurai. The master was surprised at this request, saying that his pupils usually wanted to learn how to live. The tea master told him the full story, and the master said that, as there was no time to teach him how to use the sword, the tea master should perform the tea ceremony one last time.

As this was probably the last time the tea master would be able to practise his art, he was determined to give a faultless performance. As he went through the ritual movements he achieved a degree of concentration that bordered on perfection.

The swordsman told the tea master that, when the time came for him to meet the ronin,

he was to hold his sword over his head, close his eyes and compose his mind as if he were serving tea. On hearing the ronin shout, he should cut strongly with the sword and, if all went well, the result should be a mutual death that would preserve his lord's honour. Thanking the teacher for his instruction, the tea master set off to meet his fate.

When he met the ronin, the tea master bowed and prepared to fight according to the advice he had received. He waited with his eyes closed for a few minutes but nothing happened. When he opened his eyes, he saw the ronin running away, casting aside his sword and begging for forgiveness.

Quite mystified by this turn of events, the tea master returned to the fencing teacher for an explanation. The sword master smiled and said that the fearlessness and concentration produced by the tea ceremony was such that the ronin knew he could not survive the encounter; by being prepared to abandon his life, the tea master had saved it, and maintained his lord's reputation.

Above: A section from the painted screen depicting the Siege of Osaka Castle in 1615, showing the wide range of mon used by samurai. The banners in the foreground bear the mon of the Ishikawa family.

The Satsuma Rebellion

One obvious use for unemployed samurai was war. Saigo Takamori and other traditionalists argued that Japan's problems would be solved, and her status as a world power increased, if they invaded Korea, which had provided them with an excuse by breaking off trade relations with Japan in 1873.

The plan was rejected by Iwakura Tomomi (1825-83) and his supporters, who had just returned from a mission to the United States and Europe. They knew that Japan was not yet strong enough to embark on foreign adventures and any attack on Korea would be doomed to failure. Saigo Takamori resigned from the government in disgust.

Samurai discontent increased and, as they had always done, they looked to their swords to achieve their aims. In 1874, Eto Shimpei led 2000 Kyushu samurai in revolt, until he was captured and beheaded. The commutation of samurai pensions in 1876, led to another series of revolts, which the government suppressed.

Then, in 1877, some of Saigo Takamori's followers seized a number of government arsenals in Kagoshima, without Saigo's knowledge. He was angry at first, but later accepted that it had to happen sooner or later. Firmly convinced that his army of samurai could easily deal with a force of conscripted soldiers, Saigo equipped his men with a mixture of modern and traditional arms and marched out to capture the stronghold of Kumamoto Castle, held by General Tani and around 4000 troops, most of whom were from Kyushu.

Saigo's forces laid siege to the castle for 20 days but could not force the defenders to surrender. The main imperial army relieved the castle on April 14, and engaged Saigo's forces in battle, forcing them back into Satsuma. Saigo's home base of Kagoshima, which he had left undefended, was attacked by units of the imperial navy and taken by government troops. Saigo's troops were pursued back to Kagoshima and, although they fought all the way, the superiority of government numbers and weapons wore them down, until only a few hundred warriors were left.

The final conflict

At the end, Saigo and his small group of supporters withdrew to a small cave behind Shiroyama, a hill to the north of Kagoshima. Yamagata Aritomo, the commanding general of the imperial forces and Saigo's friend, wrote to him, asking him to end his resistance.

In his letter he wrote: 'Several months have already passed since hostilities began. There have been many hundreds of casualties every day. Kinsmen are killing one another. Friends are fighting against one another... and no

Below: A carefully posed group of samurai from the time of the Satsuma Rebellion.
Note the variety of dress, from traditional samurai costume to the Western-style military uniforms.

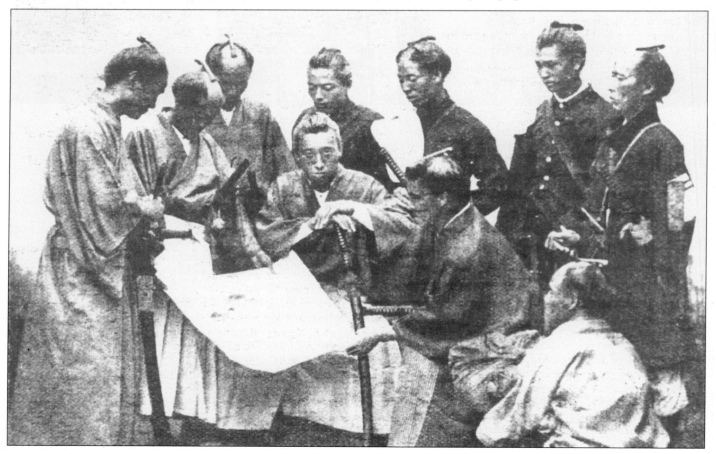

soldier on either side has any grudge against the other. His Majesty's soldiers say that they are fighting in order to fulfil their military duties, while your Satsuma men are fighting for the sake of Saigo.

'But it is evident that the Satsuma men cannot hope to accomplish their purpose, for almost all the bravest of your officers have been killed or wounded.... I earnestly entreat you to make the best of the sad situation yourself as early as you can, so as, on the one hand, to prove that the present disturbance is not of your intention and, on the other, to see to it that you may put an end to the casualties on both sides immediately. If you can successfully work out remedial measures, hostilities will soon come to an end'.

The letter had no effect. Saigo was a samurai, and surrender was not a word he understood. As Saigo and his men waited, 30,000 government troops closed in on them. At four o'clock in the morning of September 24, Saigo and his men began to move down the hill under heavy fire to attack the government troops. Saigo was hit in the groin by a bullet and could go no further.

His loyal follower Beppu Shinsuke carried him down the hill until they came to the gate of a Shimizu mansion, where Saigo sat for a few moments and then cut open his abdomen with his sword. Beppu removed his head with one cut and then charged into the imperial troops, who killed him with rifle fire. Saigo's head was recovered and washed before it was presented to General Yamagata, who bowed to it respectfully.

The last samurai

When Saigo's remains were buried, many of the government troops attending the funeral wept; he may have been an enemy, but the samurai virtues he exemplified were still highly respected.

Saigo Takamori was the last of the samurai, and with his death ended a tradition of active samurai warriors that had survived for over 1000 years. However the spirit of the samurai did not die; it was preserved by men of samurai descent to give meaning to their lives and as a guide to the shapers of modern Japan.

Perhaps the best epitaph for the samurai was written centuries before their actual passing, by the great poet Matsuo Basho, himself the son of a samurai. In 1689, he left his home and embarked on a journey that lasted two and a half years. He visited many places in the north of Japan, including the hills known as Takadate where Yoshitsune — the greatest samurai of them all — had met his death. As he gazed at the ruins of Izama-ga-shira Castle, his eyes ran with tears, and he was moved to write:
'Summer grasses —
All that remains
Of a warrior's dreams'.

Above: Often referred to as the 'last of the samurai', Saigo Takamori led the Satsuma Rebellion of 1877 against the reforming policies of the Meiji Government.

Left: In this print by Yoshitoshi a warrior defies the modern bullets during the Satsuma Rebellion.

The Samurai Legacy

Below: The Mitsui building of 1872 shows the enormous changes in Japan's skyline as a result of early modernisation. The Mitsui were already a well-established merchant family when this was built. The founder, a far-sighted samurai who saw the effects that the Tokugawa peace would have on his clan, became a merchant in the 1600s. His family continues to prosper to the present day.

Change and Continuity

The final decades of the 19th century saw Japan engaged in a massive effort of modernisation, encompassing the establishment of a Western-style constitution, universal compulsory education and the industrialisation of the economy.

Despite fierce opposition from the likes of Saigo Takamori, many samurai accepted the changes as necessary sacrifices. The example of China, at that time quite incapable of resisting exploitation by the West, presented a dire warning to Japan. Realising that their best defence lay in internal stability and modernisation, many samurai supported the Meiji government as it set about the transformation of Japan. The government's primary objective during this period was renegotiation of the hated treaties that had re-opened Japan to the West: by 1897, the treaties had been revised, and over the next decade, military victories against China and Russia gained Japan a reputation as a power to be reckoned with.

However, those samurai who had hoped that the decline of their class might also be reversed were disappointed. A samurai council set up in 1868 never reconvened after 1870, and samurai seeking to enter the Meiji bureaucracy were obliged to abandon traditional loyalties to their domain in favour of whole-hearted loyalty to the centralised state.

Nevertheless, there was continuity between the old feudal system and the modern centralised state. The outward transformation of Japanese politics concealed a continuation of clan-based politics, whose roots were very much in the samurai tradition. Japan's political reformation was led by the Choshu and Satsuma clans, and samurai from these two clans dominated the government, army and civil service during the 1870s and 1880s.

Samurai factionalism survived into the party system established in the 1890s. Osaki Yukio (1859-1954), a leading politician at the turn of the century, described the new political parties as 'affairs of personal connections and sentiments... similar to those which subsisted between a feudal lord and his liegemen'.

Continuity with the samurai past was not confined to high politics. The samurai were the best educated group in Japanese society and the absorption of Western technology depended on their active cooperation. Samurai such as Sakuma Shozan (1811-64) propounded the idea of 'Eastern ethics and Western science' ('Touo no dotoku, Seiyo no gakugei'), a blend which proved attractive to many Japanese.

Many of the earliest entrepreneurs were from samurai backgrounds. Iwasaki Yotaro (1834-85), a retainer of the Tosa clan, had been responsible for administering his clan's mercantile concerns in Nagasaki. After his domain was abolished, he ran the business as a private company. The Meiji government entrusted him with some of its financial and commercial business, and the company grew into one of the most powerful companies in Japan: Mitsubishi.

SURVIVING TRADITIONS

I n 1937, a Western observer of Japan's armed forces made much of the 'incomparable' fighting spirit of the Japanese troops. He also noted their extreme simplicity. On meeting a high-ranking officer in the War department, he was surprised to find him 'sitting unshaved in a tiny room with the dingiest kind of furniture. But this officer... was living up to the code of Bushido.... which prescribes self-denial and abstinence from ornamentation as virtues of a warrior'.

The leaders of Japan's armed forces promoted the traditions of the samurai as an example to all of Japan's soldiers, whatever their origins. The belief that death was preferable to defeat or capture was prominent during World War II. In addition to the infamous kami-kaze suicide missions made by Japanese pilots, many Japanese soldiers died in futile suicide charges or killed themselves rather than surrender.

One young lieutenant, on being taken prisoner in Burma, refused to believe that any Japanese officer had ever been taken prisoner before and pleaded with his captors to allow him an honourable death that would exonerate him from the shame of capture. Another lieutenant, due for posting to the Philippines, was given his family's historic dagger before he left. 'If you are taken captive', his mother told him, 'use this to kill yourself'. In the event, the young soldier — Hiroo Onada — did not use the dagger upon himself. Instead, together with his comrade, Kunishichi Kozuka, Onada held out in the mountains of Lubang Island long after his country had surrendered.

For 30 years, the two fought a lonely battle against the reality of Japan's defeat, and it was not until 1974, two years after his comrade's death, that Onada finally accepted that the war was over and surrendered his arms.

Left: A Japanese pilot of World War II appears on this wartime magazine cover, samurai sword in hand.

New loyalties

To bolster its support during the decades of transformation, the Meiji regime called upon a new cultural force: National Shinto. After the establishment of universal compulsory education in the 1890s, the nationalist doctrines of National Shinto — worship of the emperor, the uniqueness and superiority of the Japanese people — were spread systematically throughout Japanese society. The Way of the Warrior was enlisted in this process and held up to the Japanese people as an exemplary system of devotion.

The propagation of this creed contributed to a climate of fervent nationalism that was to bear terrible fruit during the first half of the 20th century.

In the 1930s, civilian government was hijacked by military leaders committed to military expansion. Under their regime, the twin creeds of Shinto and Bushido were used to sanction the ruthless methods by which Japan pursued its expansionist policies and, later, the atrocities committed against defeated nations and prisoners-of-war during World War II.

DIE SAMURAI

von

heinz Corazza

Left: The cover of a book published in Berlin in 1943, idealising the samurai spirit of Germany's wartime ally. Note the Japanese naval standard carried by the samurai.

The Last Great Swordsman

The martial arts developed by the samurai were deemed their finest legacy and it is by looking at their continuing history that we can best see the surviving samurai tradition. An important figure in the transmission of samurai martial arts to a wider following was Yamaoka Tesshu.

Tesshu is often called the last of the great swordsmen. He was representative of a generation of masters who were able to spread formerly exclusive systems to non-samurai practitioners without losing their true meaning and martial spirit.

Yamaoka Tesshu was born into a samurai family in 1836. It was his father who first introduced him to the art of the sword, and he later became a student of a famous swordsman, Chiba Shusaku, who taught him the Hokushin Itto Ryu. At the age of 20, Tesshu was adopted into the Yamaoka family, having married Yamaoka Fusako in 1855.

Below: Yamaoka Tesshu, the last great swordsman of Japan.

At this time, as Tesshu was learning the Yamaoka style of spear fighting (So-jutsu), many of the martial arts dojos became gathering places for young samurai who were deeply committed to the sonno-joi movement and Tesshu became involved in the political ferment of the young shishi.

Although Tesshu sympathised with the aims of the sonno-joi movement, during the conflicts that preceded the Meiji Restoration he acted on behalf of the Tokugawa shogunate. On one occasion, the young Tesshu met Saigo Takamori, coolly walking through the imperial lines and into Saigo's headquarters to deliver the great general a message from the Tokugawa forces.

After the Meiji Restoration, he was employed by the government, eventually being honoured with the rank of viscount. His lifelong study of Zen Buddhism and the martial arts led to the creation of his own school of swordsmanship, which he called 'Muto Ryu' ('No-Sword School'). In his own dojo, the Shumpukan (The Hall of the Spring Wind — the name was taken from a poem by the 13th-century Zen-master, Bukko Kokushi) Tesshu began teaching his distinctive method to his students.

Tesshu's method

Tesshu believed that swordsmanship 'should lead directly to the heart of things where one can directly confront life and death. Recently, swordsmanship has become a mere pastime with no bearing on matters of importance'. The method Tesshu devised was extraordinarily demanding, pushing his students to the limits of their endurance.

He devised three tests, called seigan — a Buddhist term meaning vow. These could only be taken by advanced students. After 1000 consecutive days of practice, the candidate could take the first test, which consisted of 200 contests with only a short pause for food. If successful, the candidate was eligible for the second test: 600 contests over a period of three days. The third seigan was the ultimate test: 1400 contests over seven days, pushing the candidate into realms where physical skills alone were not enough. To succeed at the third seigan, swordsmen had to unite all their physical and spiritual strength with an absolute acceptance that victory or death could be their only choices.

For Tesshu, the true function of the martial arts was to develop the spirit; they were a shugyo (austere discipline), whose purpose was not simply the destruction of an enemy but the forging of spiritual strength in the practitioner.

As a young man, Tesshu struggled for years to strengthen both his body and his spirit, training with such ferocity that he was nicknamed 'demon', and overcoming all his opponents. Then, when Tesshu was 28, he faced Asari Gimei in a match. Asari was a master of the Nakanishi-ha Itto Ryu style of swordsmanship, and although Tesshu attacked with all his strength, he was unable to make any impression on his opponent. He became Asari's student, but in subsequent matches he was unable to penetrate Asari's defences and was soundly defeated time after time.

'Pierce the Heavens!'

Tesshu was determined to find some way of defeating his new teacher and sought the help of Tekisui, the abbot of Tenruji. Tekisui gave Tesshu a koan to study and meditate on:

'When two flashing swords meet there is no place to escape,
Move on coolly, like a lotus flower blooming in the midst of a roaring fire
And forcefully pierce the Heavens!'.

At the age of 45, while sitting in meditation, Tesshu finally grasped the meaning of Tekisui's koan. He went to see his teacher, Asari Gimei, to put his enlightenment to the test, but as soon as they crossed swords, Asari let his blade drop, exclaiming: 'You have arrived'. Later, Asari designated Tesshu his successor as headmaster of the Nakanishi-ha Itto Ryu.

In the years since Tesshu's death in 1888, modern martial artists have been greatly influenced by Tesshu's ideas, and one karate master, Oyama Masatatsu, has adapted Tesshu's seigan to his own school of karate. Practitioners of Kyokushinkai karate can, if they wish and are strong enough, engage in 100 contests without pause as a test of their physical and mental conditioning.

Many systems of traditional martial arts have special training sessions in the depths of winter, where practitioners can measure their fortitude against the numbing effects of snow, ice and freezing water. A common practice for some karate styles is to perform the formal exercise (kata) of sanchin (three battles) while standing under a waterfall fed by melting snow.

Left: At this kendo tournament in 1925 the swordsman Kurahashi is dressed up in full 16th-century armour, to the evident fascination of his audience.

The Martial Arts

It is through the medium of the martial arts that many of the samurai values and beliefs have been transmitted to non-Japanese cultures, so preserving some aspects of the samurai legacy outside Japan.

Japanese martial arts are now practised world wide as methods of self-defence, self-discipline and sport. While the classical systems of swordsmanship and related methods attract a devoted following, the systems of judo, karate-do, kendo and aikido are the most popular, and highly skilled non-Japanese teachers and practitioners can be found in countries throughout the world.

Judo

Below: A page from Hokusai's 'Manga' ('Sketchbook') showing a variety of ju-jutsu holds applied to the elbow.

Judo was described by its founder Kano Jigoro (1860-1938) as 'The Way of Gentleness, or of first giving way in order to ultimately gain the victory'. Kano originally studied a number of ju-jutsu styles, principally Tenjin Shinyo Ryu and Kito Ryu, and began to teach his own

synthesis of ju-jutsu techniques allied to ideas and methods taken from Western sports, such as gymnastics, in 1882.

Kano intended that his art of judo should preserve the best of classical ju-jutsu, and that it should be more than just a sport or a method of fighting. He stressed that judo should develop not only the student's physical skills, but should also enhance the practitioner's moral values; in short, it would be a gentleman's martial art.

Judo, as it is practised today, is a contest sport in which the aim is to throw or lock an opponent according to strictly defined rules. The martial element has gradually declined due to the stress on sporting considerations, a trend which was strengthened when judo became an Olympic event in 1964.

Karate-do

Karate-do (The Empty Hand Way) entered Japan at the beginning of this century. Originally an Okinawan style, known as Te (hand), karate was brought to Japan by an Okinawan schoolteacher named Funakoshi Gichin (1868-1957).

Karate stresses kicking and punching, although some styles also teach throwing techniques, arm and wrist locks, and the use of traditional Okinawan weapons, such as the staff (bo), jointed flail (nunchaku) or knuckle dusters (tekko).

Following the example of judo, Funakoshi Gichin and other karate-do masters wanted karate to be seen as something more than simply a method of fighting. The development of a strong fighting spirit was important, but this had to be accompanied by an equally strong spiritual and moral element to avoid the misuse of the art.

Funakoshi Gichin wrote a code of 20 precepts, among which he said: 'Karate begins and ends with courtesy'; 'There is no first attack in karate'; and 'Karate is an auxiliary of justice'. The teachings and practices of the arts of the sword were applied to the art of the empty hand, so karate became a means of preserving and developing the samurai spirit. In the West, karate is most commonly taught as a sport but the older ideals of self-defence and self-discipline still have many followers.

Kendo

Kendo (The Way of the Sword) is very popular in Japan and has a growing number of followers in the West. Generally, kendo is taught as a system of sporting combat, in which the practitioners wear protective armour and try to score points on designated targets with a bamboo sword (or shinai).

Derived from the older classical systems of swordsmanship, kendo practitioners generally regard the sporting aspect of their art as the least important part of the discipline. It is

Left: Modern karate, one of the most popular of the martial arts based on actual fighting techniques from Japan's past.

common for kendo practitioners to also train in ken-jutsu, which features training with a real blade in techniques designed to dispatch an enemy as quickly and effectively as possible. The methods taught by the older ken-jutsu styles are the same techniques as taught to the samurai, and are based on the conditions and circumstances likely to be faced by a samurai on the field of battle.

Some of the kata (formal exercises) taught by one of the oldest ken-jutsu schools, the Tenshin Shoden Katori Shino Ryu, teach the practitioner to direct his cuts at the vulnerable points of an opponent's armour. These systems have no place on the modern battlefield or in sporting competitions, but survive as living examples of the methods used by the samurai.

Aikido

Aikido (The Way of Harmony) was created by Uyeshiba Morihei (1883-1969). As a young man, Uyeshiba studied a number of ju-jutsu systems, as well as swordsmanship and spear fighting. He became a student of Takeda Sikaku, a stern traditionalist and headmaster of the Daito Ryu (a combat method that had been taught for centuries to the samurai to the Takeda clan).

By combining the various arts of combat he had studied with a range of ideas and concepts drawn from the Omotokyo sect, a sect rooted in nature worship and spirit possession, Uyeshiba established his own system of fighting and self discipline.

According to Uyeshiba, the true spirit of the martial arts was revealed to him in 1925, as he was walking in a garden. 'Golden vapour gushed out of the earth... and I felt myself turning into a golden body.... It was precisely at

that moment that I received enlightenment.... martial training is not training that has as its primary purpose the defeating of others, but practice of God's love within ourselves'.

The techniques of aikido feature rapid turning movements, designed to blend with an attacker's movements so as to throw or unbalance him. An aikido master is often compared to the eye of a hurricane; quiet in himself but difficult to approach because of the tremendous forces swirling around him.

Below: A children's kendo class in action - with the samurai of tomorrow?

THE TIES THAT BIND

For a samurai, loyalty or duty to his lord and clan was everything. Known as giri in Japanese, loyalty was at the heart of a samurai's relationship with his lord. The obligations incurred when a samurai entered a lord's service demanded that, in return for the lord's protection, he should willingly sacrifice everything, including his life, to protect his lord's interests.

This attitude developed early among the samurai. Tameyoshi, the grandfather of Minamoto Yoritomo (1147-98) was once called to the court of a cloistered emperor. He spoke to the emperor, explaining: 'I come because I have been told to come by the head of my

Below: In this print we see the loyal 19 retainers of Minamoto Yoshitsune, who accompanied him at his battles and on his wanderings, exemplars of the fidelity to one's master that was a hallmark of the samurai code.

house. Otherwise, not even an imperial edict could bring me to the palace, for we Minamoto do not serve two masters'.

The writers who defined samurai codes under the Tokugawa shoguns placed considerable emphasis on giri. To Yamaga Soko, the role of the warrior class 'consists in reflecting on his own station in life, in discharging loyal service to his master... deepening his fidelity in associations with friends, and in devoting himself to duty above all.... Should there be someone in the three classes of the common people who transgresses against these moral principles, the samurai summarily punishes him and upholds proper moral principles in the land'.

Tragedy in Japanese drama is often the result of the clash of giri with ninjo (human feelings). A typical story might deal with the love between a young samurai and a courtesan who are doomed because of the wide social gulf which separates them. Usually one or both will kill themselves in order to resolve the impasse, or the girl will reject her suitor so as not to blight his future, sometimes spending the remainder of her life doing good works as a Buddhist nun.

Punishing disloyalty

A classic story of giri is to be found in the 'Honcho Bugei Shoden' ('A Survey of the Martial Arts'), written in 1714 by Hinatsu Shirozaemon Shigetaka. Moro-oka Ippa was a teacher of swordsmanship derived from the Katori Shinto Ryu. He had three talented pupils, Negishi Tokaku, Iwama Koguma and Tsuchko Doronosuke. When Moro-oka contracted leprosy, Iwama and Tsuchiko devoted themselves to their master's welfare, selling their possessions and pawning their swords to buy him medicines, but Negishi Tokaku refused to help his teacher and ran away to Odawara, in Musashi province. There, he became very successful, teaching a style of swordsmanship based on his master's methods, which he called Mijin Ryu.

Three years later, Moro-oka Ippa died and Negishi, who had since moved to Edo, proclaimed himself heir to his martial tradition. Iwama and Tsuchiko swore to punish Negishi for ignoring his obligations to his master, and they journeyed together to the Kashima shrine to pray for divine aid in their vendetta. Tsuchiko submitted a petition to the shrine in which he pledged that, if their mission failed: 'I shall return alive to this shrine... cut open my stomach, and with my foul blood stain the sacred pillar red. I will become an evil spirit, forever haunting the shrine's garden... as a demon-fox'.

Left: In this Meiji photograph we may note the requirements of etiquette stipulated between two equally ranking samurai, which has ensured that each bows his head the same distance towards the ground as the other.

When Iwama arrived in Edo and challenged Negishi to fight, Tokugawa Ieyasu heard about the match and gave his permission for the men to meet on Tokiwa bridge. Supremely confident, Negishi Tokaku arrived with a large retinue of his students who had come to see their master destroy Iwama Koguma. Facing each other with wooden swords, they rushed together in the centre of the bridge. Negishi made a cut at Iwama's head, but Iwama closed with him, seized him by the legs and threw him into the river.

After Negishi's defeat, his students abandoned him for Iwama Koguma, who became the true heir of Moro-oka Ippa's style of swordsmanship.

Strategic betrayals

During the Sengoku Jidai, the ideal of loyalty was frequently overruled by political considerations. Akechi Mitsuhide said that lies were part of a warrior's strategy, a teaching he put into practice when he turned on his own lord, Nobunaga, and killed him. Takeda Shingen's younger brother was the author of a set of observations designed to help the Takeda samurai and their vassals. 'The samurai must never relax his guard' he wrote. 'Even when alone with his wife, he should... have his sword at hand'.

This observation was echoed by Mori Motonari, a Sengoku Jidai warlord whose family dominated western Japan after the Battle of Miyajima in 1555, who maintained that even close relatives should not be trusted. But the value of loyalty was not wholly ignored by the warlords of the Sengoku Jidai. According to one well-known story, Moto Motonari once gave each of his three sons a single arrow and invited them to break it. He then gave them three arrows, to show how difficult it was to break the arrows when they were held together.

The lesson was not lost on the sons, whose families remained loyal to one another for many years.

The emphasis on duty did not prevent a warrior from admiring a brave opponent. During the Russo-Japanese War of 1904-05, the Russian fleet under Admiral Rodjesvensky was destroyed by a Japanese fleet commanded by Admiral Togo. Admiral Togo visited his defeated opponent as he lay badly wounded in the destroyer Biedovy. Speaking very gently, he told Rodjesvensky: 'Defeat can be the fate of any one of us. What counts is to have done one's duty'.

Below: The 'Parable of the Arrows', whereby Mori Motonari demonstrated the virtues of loyalty and solidarity to his sons.

Modern Japan

Right: A moment from one of the many jidai-matsuri (festivals of the ages) now held in Japan, where visitors can see re-enactments of Japan's samurai past. This particular one is held in Nagoya.

Modern cities shuffle national identities like cards in a pack. Just as London, Paris and New York now have sushi bars and karaoke machines, so visitors to modern Tokyo see people dressed in fashionable Western-style clothes; eating foods from haute-cuisine to MacDonalds; playing golf and baseball; and listening to Western music.

But the adoption of Western culture, like the adoption of Chinese culture in the 6th century, has been undertaken on Japan's own terms. Japan remains a deeply conservative society. For example, although guaranteed equal rights under the 1947 constitution, women obtain more marginal jobs and receive smaller wages than men. Their opportunities are still constrained by traditional roles that were first defined by the samurai.

Traditions of group loyalty still dominate Japanese society. Successive corruption scandals concerning leading politicians reflect the continuation of faction-based politics; and in schools, universities, sports clubs and the workplace, group identities continue to hold sway. These hierarchical structures are essentially the same as those which existed in villages before industrialisation and echo the relationships that the samurai made central to their existence.

Below: A young Japanese woman kneels at the grave of one of the 47 Ronin, in the Sengakuji temple in Tokyo.

Time and again, the Japanese turn to their samurai past in defining their national identity. This process often takes a humorous form; in the 1980s, the samurai emphasis on stoic endurance (known as ganban) provided the basis for a spectacular game show, 'Za Ganban', in which teams of volunteer victims endured a

'BUSINESS WARRIORS'

'Now the secret of Japanese success in business can be yours. It lies within the pages of this age-old masterpiece of winning strategy'. So ran the publisher's hype for a recent US publication of Miyamoto Musashi's 'The Book of Five Rings'. In a context of recurrent conflicts over trade tariffs, Western observers, viewing Japanese business as war by another means, regularly seize upon its martial heritage to explain its success. But this perception is not confined to the West; the image of the modern-day 'business warrior' is also common in Japan.

Success has generated numerous myths about Japanese business; some of the management practices that have been singled out as distinctively Japanese in fact originated in the US (just-in-time inventories, for example). Nevertheless, there is a basis for the samurai connection. The keen sense of the national interest that underpinned Japan's first business revolution can be traced to the influence of samurai entrepreneurs from the Meiji era. Indeed, many of the features of Japanese business most envied by the West (the value placed on education; the importance of hierarchy; the promotion of group identity) are rooted in traditional samurai values.

These values are often inculcated by traditional samurai means. Management training schemes in some big companies still follow the Zen-inspired traditions of the samurai past, requiring new recruits to live in a company dormitory for a couple of months, during which they are expected to perform communal tasks and obey a curfew.

Like the samurai, the modern 'salary-man' is valued by his company for his loyalty. Promotion generally depends more on the length of time a worker has served in a company than on individual successes. In return, the company (at least in big organisations) looks after the interests of its employees, giving them priority over the interests of shareholders, protecting their job security as far as possible, and working to secure alternative positions for staff they have had to make redundant. Many companies only provide such support to their full-time workers, while the larger proportion of their workforces are part-time. But as an ideal, if not always as a practice, the code of mutual obligations has clearly outlived the warrior class that first propagated it in feudal Japan.

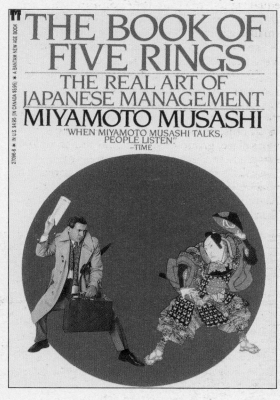

Left: 'The real art of Japanese management'? The image of a medieval samurai takes on an American businessman on the cover of this US edition of Miyamoto Musashi's 'The Book of Five Rings'.

series of increasingly elaborate tortures, much to the delight of a huge TV audience.

Samurai appear in comics and adverts, and historical epics dramatising the samurai past are a staple of TV. Cinema regularly returns to the samurai for its subject matter. Films such as Kurosawa's 'Seven Samurai' (remade in the US as 'The Magnificent Seven') or 'Ran', evoke a past of heroism, endurance and honour, while at the same time satisfying the Japanese appetite for on-screen violence.

The attractions of samurai history to extreme nationalists have been reaffirmed in recent years. Yukio Mishima, one of Japan's great post-war novelists, frequently placed his novels in the samurai age. He was also a founding member of a far-right political group that celebrated samurai traditions in their call for a renewal of Japanese militarism.

But the story of Mishima's botched ritual suicide in 1970, which conspicuously failed to rally nationalist sympathies (the armed forces were particularly unimpressed), indicates a fundamental change in Japanese attitudes to their military past. The 'samurai' of modern Japan are more often cultural ambassadors than sabre-rattlers. The Japan Festival staged in London in 1991 was an exercise in cultural diplomacy that gave pride of place, alongside sumo wrestlers and the latest computer technology, to an historical re-enactment group performing spectacular displays of the samurai martial arts, dressed in the glittering costume of their legendary forbears.

Glossary

Aikido	The Way of Harmony.
Ainu	Indigenous inhabitants of Japan.
Akuso	'Bad monks' recruited as guards by Buddhist sects.
Ashigaru	'Light feet' — peasant troops.
Bakufu	'Camp office' — shogun's government.
Bushido	The Way of the Warrior.
Daimyo	Powerful feudal landowner.
Daisho	The two swords worn by samurai.
Daito	Swords over 61 cm (2 ft) long.
Dojo	Place for teaching martial arts.
Fumi-e	Device used to trap Christians.
Gekokujo	'The low oppress the high' — social unrest during the Sengoku Jidai.
Giri	Duty or obligation.
Gunpai	Metal war fan.
Hara-kiri	Suicide by cutting into stomach.
Ikki	Armed peasant league.
Ikko-ikki	'Single-minded League' — 15th-century militant religious group.
Jitte	Short iron bar with a prong on one side.
Judo	The Art of Gentleness.
Junshi	Seppuku performed upon a lord's death.
Kaishakunin	Assistant during act of seppuku.
Kami-kaze	'Divine wind' — storms which destroyed Mongol fleet.
Kami	Spirits and gods.
Kampaku	Regent.
Kanshi	Seppuku performed as remonstrance to a superior.
Karate-do	The Way of the Empty Hand.
Katsujin no ken	'The Sword that gives Life'. Character-forming aspect of the martial arts.
Kendo	The Way of the Sword. Fencing method developed from ken-jutsu.
Ken-jutsu	The Art of the Sword. Sword-fighting techniques used in battle.
Kirisutogomen	Samurai right to cut down disrespectful members of a lower class.
Kishin	Tax exemption.
Koku	Measurement of wealth, usually defined as the amount of rice needed to feed a man for a year.
Kusari-gama	Weapon, comprising chain and sickle.
Kyuba no michi	The Way of the Horse and Bow. Early warrior code. Also known as Kyusen no Michi (The Way of the Bow and Arrow).
Man-dokoro	Administrative organ of the bakufu.
Mikoshi	Portable Buddhist shrine.
Mon	Family crests.
Monchu-jo	Judicial body of the bakufu.
Musha-shugyo	Warrior pilgrimage.
Naginata	Pole-arm, fitted with curved single-edged blade.
Ninja	Assassins and spies; practitioners of the Art of Invisibility.
No-dachi	Long sword.
Oyoroi	Classic armour of the Heian period.
Ronin	'Wave men' — samurai without a lord.
Ryu	School of martial arts.
Samurai	Member of the warrior class; warrior in daimyo's service.
Samurai dokoro	Disciplinary body of the bakufu.
Sankin-kotai	System of 'alternate attendance' that required daimyo to attend the shogun's court.
Sashimono	Identifying banner, fitted to the back of the armour.
Satsujin no ken	'The Sword that takes Life'. The destructive aspect of the martial arts.
Seishin tanren	Spiritual forging; using martial arts for spiritual discipline.
Sengoku Jidai	'Age of the Country at War' (15th and 16th centuries).
Seppuku	Ritual suicide.
Shikken	Shogun's regent.
Shishi	'Men of High Purpose'. 19th-century xenophobic samurai.
Shoen	Large provincial estates.
Shogun	Abbreviated form of Sei-I-Tai Shogun ('barbarian subduing general').
Shugyo	Austere discipline.
So-jutsu	Spear-fighting.
Sohei	Warrior monks.
Sonno-joi	19th-century xenophobic movement opposed to the shogunate.
Tendai	School of Buddhism derived from the Chinese T'ien-t'ai sect.
Tengu	Mythical creatures, half man, half bird, expert in the martial arts.
Tsuba	Sword guard.
Uji	Family groupings that emerged in early Japanese history.
Wakizashi	Sword 30 to 61 cm (1 to 2 ft) long.
Zanshin	Ability to sense danger.
Zen	Form of Buddhism stressing direct experience above the scriptures.

Bibliography

Many sources have been used in the compilation of this book. The author acknowledges his particular debts to the following works:

Hideyoshi, M. E. Berry, Harvard University Press, 1989.

The Echigo War, H. Bolitho, Monumenta Nipponica, Vol.34/No.3.

Arms and Armour of the Samurai, I. Bottomley and A. P. Hopson, Defoe Publishing, 1988.

Samurai: The Invincible Warriors, F. Brinkley, Ohara Publications Inc., 1975.

The Satsuma Rebellion of 1877, J. H. Buck, Monumenta Nipponica, Vol.28/No.3.

Heike Monogatari and the Japanese Warrior Ethic, K. Butler, Harvard Journal of Asian Studies, Vol.29.

Tales of Samurai Honour, C. Callahan, Monumenta Nipponica, Vol.34/No.1.

The Martial Arts and Ways of Japan: Vols.1-3, D. F. Draeger, Weatherhill, 1973.

Karate-Do: My Way of Life, Gichin Fuinakoshi, Kodansha International, 1975.

Sun-Tzu: The Art of War, S. B. Griffith, Oxford University Press, 1971.

Nippon-To: The Japanese Sword, Inami Hakusui, Japan Sword Co. Ltd, Tokyo, 1948.

The Fighting Spirit of Japan, E. J. Harrison, T. Fisher Unwin, London, 1913.

Zen and Confucius in the Art of Swordsmanship, R. Kammer (trans. B. J. Fitzgerald), Routledge and Kegan Paul, 1978.

Hogen Monogatari, E. R. Kellogg, Transactions of Asiatic Society of Japan, Vol.45/No.1, 1917.

Okinawa: The History of an Island People, G. H. Kerr, Charles E. Tuttle Co., 1959.

Zen and the Ways, T. Leggett, Routledge and Kegan Paul, 1978.

The Japan Reader Vol.1, J. Livingstone, J. Moore, F. Oldfather, Penguin Books, 1976.

Autumn Lightning, D. Lowry, Shambhala Publications Inc., 1985.

The Taiheiki, H. C. McCullogh, Charles E. Tuttle Co., 1979.

The Nobility of Failure, I. Morris, Secker and Warburg Ltd., London, 1975.

Karate-Do: History and Philosophy, Takao Nakaya, JSS Publishing Co., USA, 1986.

Bushido: The Soul of Japan, Inanzo Nitobe, Kenkyusha, Tokyo, 1935.

The Deity and the Sword: Shinto Ryu Vols.1-3, Otake Risuke, Minato Research and Publishing Co. Ltd., Tokyo, 1977 and 1978.

Sons of Heaven, J. M. Packard, Macdonald Queen Anne Press, 1988.

Giving up the Gun, D. R. Godine, Publisher Inc., Boston, 1979.

Japan: Strategy of the Unseen, M. Random, Thorsons Publishing Group Ltd., 1987.

Tales of Old Japan, Lord Redesdale, Macmillan and Co., London, 1910.

The Way of the Warrior, H. Reid and M. Croucher, Century Publishing, 1983.

Japan: Tradition and Transformation (revised edition), E. O. Reischauer and A. M. Craig, Allen and Unwin, Australia, 1989.

Zen Flesh, Zen Bones, P. Reps, Penguin Books, 1982.

The Arts of the Japanese Sword, B. W. Robinson, Charles E. Tuttle Co., 1961.

Arts of War in Times of Peace, J. M. Rogers, Monumenta Nipponica Vol.45/No.3 and 4.

The Code of the Samurai, A. L. Sadler, 1941, (reprinted Charles E. Tuttle Co., 1988.).

Tales of Samurai Honour: Buke Giri Monogatari, Ihara Saikaku (trans. C. A. Callahan), Monumenta Nipponica Monograph 57, Sophia University, Tokyo, 1981.

The Samurai Disestablished, Masayoshi Sakeda and George Akita, Monumenta Nipponica Vol.41/No.3.

Sabre Contre Katana, S. Salvini, Karate no. 155.

Japan: A Short Cultural History, G. B. Sansom, Century Hutchinson Ltd., 1987.

A History of Japan 1334-1615, G. B. Sansom, Cresset Press, London, 1961.

The Elements of Zen, D. Scott and T. Doubleday, Element Books Ltd., 1992.

Hara-kiri: Japanese Ritual Suicide, J. Seward, Charles E. Tuttle Co., 1968.

The Sword of No-Sword, J. Stevens, Shambhalha Publications Inc., 1984.

The Way of the Samurai, R. Storry, Orbis Publishing, London, 1978.

Lives of the Master Swordsmen, Sugawara Makoto, The East Publications Inc., Tokyo, 1988.

Zen and Japanese Culture, D. T. Suzuki, Princeton University Press, 1973.

The Unfettered Mind, Soho Takuan (trans. W. Scott Wilson), Kodansha International, 1986.

Sources of Japanese Tradition: Vols.1-2, Ryusaku Tsunoda et al., Columbia University Press, 1964.

The Book of the Samurai, S. Turnbull, Arms and Armour Press Ltd., 1982.

The Samurai: A Military History, S. Turnbull, Macmillan Publishing Co., 1977.

Samurai Warriors, S. Turnbull, Blandford Press Ltd., 1990.

The Samurai, I. Morris, M. Morris and P. H. Varley, Penguin Books, 1974.

Japanese Swordsmanship, G. Warner and D. F. Draeger, Weatherhill, 1982.

Budoshinshu: Warrior Primer of Daidoji Yuzan, W. Scott Wilson, Ohara Publications Inc., 1984.

Ideals of the Samurai, W. Scott Wilson, Ohara Publications Inc., 1982.

Hagakure, Tsunetomo Yamamoto (trans. W. Scott Wilson), Kodansha international Ltd., 1979.

The Enigma of Japanese Power, K.van Wolferen, Macmillan, 1989.

Pink Samurai, N. Bornoff, Grafton, 1992.

The Japanese Achievement, Hugh Corzanni, Sidgwick and Jackson, 1990.

No Surrender, Hiroo Onoda, Andre Deutsch Ltd., 1975.

ACKNOWLEDGEMENTS

All efforts have been made to contact the copyright holders of any material in this book that may be in copyright, but Morgan Samuel Editions would be grateful to receive notice of any copyright material that may have been overlooked.

Morgan Samuel Editions would like to express their gratitude to the following individuals and organisations who have supplied the illustrations in this book.

p6: Mary Evans; p7: Bridgeman Art Library; p8 (bottom left): Werner Forman Archive; p8 (bottom right): Suzanne Perrin; p9 (top): Lucy Horne/Barnaby's Picture Library; p9 (bottom): E. Skelding; p10 (left): S.Perrin; p10 (right): W.F.A.; p11 (left): Japan Information Centre (Embassy of Japan); p11 (right), p12 (bottom): S.Perrin; p12 (top): Stephen Turnbull; p13: W.F.A.; p14 (top): University of Durham, Oriental Museum; p14 (bottom): W.F.A./Kozu Collection, Kyoto; p15 (top): S.Turnbull; p15 (bottom): University of Durham, Oriental Museum; p16: Imperial Household Agency, Tokyo; p17, p18 (top): W.F.A.; p18 (bottom): Edimedia; p19: W.F.A./Private Collection; p20 (top): Archiv Gerstenberg; p20 (bottom): S.Turnbull; p21: Archiv fur Kunst und Geschichte, Berlin; p22: Ancient Art and Architecture Collection; p23: Scala/Art Resource, New York; p24: Bridgeman; p25: S.Turnbull; p26: E.T.Archive; p27 (top): W.F.A.; p27 (bottom): S. Turnbull; p28: S.Perrin; p29 (top and bottom): S.Turnbull; p30: S.Perrin; p31, p32 (top and bottom): S.Turnbull; p33 (top): W.F.A./Ninja Museum, Ueno; p33 (bottom): S.Turnbull; p34: W.F.A./Boston Museum of Fine Arts; p35 (top): Edimedia; p35 (bottom): S.Turnbull; p36: W.F.A./Boston Museum of Fine Arts; p37: Edimedia; p38 (top): University of Durham, Oriental Museum; p38 (bottom): S.Turnbull; p39: Edimedia; p40: S.Turnbull; p41: Bridgeman; p42: Peter Newark; p43: S.Turnbull; p44: Bridgeman; p45 (top): Peter Newark; p45 (bottom): Archiv Gerstenberg; pp46/7: S.Turnbull; p48 (top): Bridgeman; p48 (bottom): S.Turnbull; p49: Archiv Gerstenberg; p50: Archiv fur Kunst und Geschichte; p51 (top): S.Turnbull; p52 (top): S.Perrin; p52 (bottom): Archiv fur Kunst und Geschichte; p53 (top): S.Turnbull; p52 (bottom): Archive fur Kunst und Geschichte; p53: S.Perrin; p54: Bridgeman; p55 (top): E.T.Archive; p55 (bottom): Mansell Collection; p56, p57 (top): S.Turnbull; p57 (bottom): Bridgeman; p58 (top): Edimedia; p58 (bottom): Archiv fur Kunst und Geschichte; p59: E.T.Archive; p60: Manchester Museum; p61 (top): W.F.A.; p61 (bottom), p62 (top), p63: S.Turnbull; p62 (bottom): W.F.A.; pp64 (top): Bridgeman; p64 (bottom left): Edimedia; pp64 (right), 65: S.Turnbull; p66 (top):University of Durham, Oriental Museum; p66 (bottom): E.T.Archive; p67 (top): S.Turnbull; p67 (bottom): W.F.A.; p68: Museo Stibbert Firenze/Art Resource; p69 (top): Archiv Gerstenberg; p69 (bottom), p70: Ancient Art and Architecture Collection; p71 (top): W.F.A.; p71 (bottom): S.Turnbull; p72: V&A; p73: W.F.A.; p74, p75 (bottom): S.Turnbull; p75 (top): Archiv fur Kunst und Geschichte; p76 (top): Japanese National Tourist Organisation; p76 (bottom), p77, p78: S.Turnbull; p79: Archiv fur Kunst und Geschichte; pp80/1, 82/3, 84/5, 86 (bottom): S.Turnbull; p86 (top), p87 (right): W.F.A.; p87 (left): Mansell; p88, p89 (top):S.Turnbull; p89 (bottom): S.Perrin; p90: S.Perrin; p91: W.F.A.; p92: Japanese National Tourist Organisation; p93: P.Newark; pp94/5, 96/7, 98/9: S.Turnbull; p100 (top): Japan Information Centre; p100 (bottom): William McQuitty; p101: W.F.A.; p102: Archive fur Kunst und Geschichte; p103 (top): S.Turnbull; p103 (bottom): W.F.A.; p104: S.Turnbull; p105: Japanese National Tourist Organisation; p106, 107 (bottom): S.Turnbull; p107 (top): Tokugawa Art Museum; p108, 109: V&A; p110 (right): Archive fur Kunst und Geschichte; p110, 111, 112: S.Turnbull; p113 (top): S.Perrin; p113 (bottom): V&A; p114: S.Turnbull; p115 (top): V&A; p115 (bottom): E.Skelding; pp116, 117 (top): Mansell Collection; p117 (bottom): Peter Newark; p118: S.Turnbull; p119: E.T.Archive; p120 (top): Edimedia; p120 (bottom): Illustrated London News; p121: S.Turnbull; p122: S.Perrin; p123 (top): Mansell Collection; p123 (bottom): E.T.Archive; p124: Archiv Gerstenberg; p125: W.F.A.; p126: Peter Newark; p127: S.Turnbull; p128, 129 (top): Peter Newark; p129 (bottom): Archiv fur Kunst und Geschichte; p130: John Stevens; p131: Archiv fur Kunst und Geschichte; p132: V&A; p133 (top): E. Skelding; p133 (bottom): S.Perrin; p134: Archiv Gerstenberg; p135 (top): Edimedia; p135 (bottom): S.Turnbull; p136 (top): S.Perrin; p136 (bottom): E. Skelding; p137: From 'The Book of Five Rings' by Miyamoto Musashi. Copyright (c) 1982 by Bantam, a division of Bantam Doubleday Dell Publishing Group, Inc. Used by permission of Bantam Books, a division of Bantam Doubleday Dell Publishing Group, Inc.

Editor:	Robert Saunders
Editorial Assistance:	Martina Stansbie
Picture Researcher:	Dee Robinson
Indexer:	Robert Saunders
Designer:	Ian Sheppard
Typesetting & Reprographics:	PrePress Ltd, London
Production Manager:	Pip Morgan
Publisher:	Nigel Perryman

In addition, Morgan Samuel Editions would like to express their gratitude for the generous assistance of Stephen Turnbull, Suzanne Perrin and Sophie Davies, without whom this publication would not have been possible.